A Eulogy to the Cosmos

Seeing the Divine through the Eyes of a

Quantum World

H.L. Sawyer

Dedication

For mom and dad…. the kindest people I have ever known. In the lottery that is life, I hit the jackpot being born to them. Thanks for all you gave to me.

Acknowledgment

I want to acknowledge the writings of both Rhonda Byrne and Dr. Robert Lanza.

Ms. Byrne's book, The Greatest Secret, opened my eyes to the concept of Awareness, an eternal force that created our Universe and resides within all things. I was immediately intrigued by using the verbiage of Awareness instead of God. Aware(ness) is both an adjective and a noun. Awareness as a noun is the state of being aware. Being aware is an adjective; having knowledge of something. Since the Creator is beyond definition, I found using both a noun and an adjective to define Godly processes to be more malleable. Also, the term God comes with many preconditions that Awareness is not encumbered by. I am sure there is an overlap between my writings and Ms. Byrne's, but I am equally sure my interpretation of Awareness (God) I have made my own.

In his book Biocentrism, Dr. Robert Lanza presents a complex argument about how life and consciousness are key drivers in the Universe. He presents the concept that life is a projection of our conscious minds. While at times I became a little lost, his writing is magnificent. He introduced me to the quantum world and how it defies traditional laws of physics. Dr Lanza opened my eyes to the real prospect that our relationship with the Divine may very well mirror the mechanics of the quantum world.

Thank you to both of you.

Finally, I also must acknowledge there were many snippets that I took from the internet in bits and pieces that I used when compiling and verifying my words and thoughts. They became a primordial ooze of sorts, from which I cut and pasted my thoughts after running them through the filter of my Awareness. It was a very messy process.

CONTENTS

About the Author

Hugo Lux Sawyer is a self-professed 'regular guy' and a bit of a character. HL never focused on any specific career path. Instead, he opted to pursue happiness as his ultimate journey in life.

Upon graduating the George Washington University in Washington DC, he briefly lived in a commune in the Poconos mountains. From there, he literally threw a dart at a map and hit Maine as his next destination.

In Maine, he found a home on Peaks Island, a small community off the coast of Portland, accessible only by boat. On Peaks Island he found his lifelong love, Denise, and started a family together. He worked as both a social worker and a construction worker. After eight happy years, the long Maine winters proved too much, and he opted to move to the South.

H.L. being a free spirit, opted to try something totally new. He decided to build a Par 3 golf course and driving range with his brother as a silent partner. After an extensive search he ended up just outside Charleston S.C.

H.L. turned his odd adventure into a reality and MacDuffer's Par 3/Driving Range opened for business. He operated the facility for ten years before selling his interest to his brother.

He then returned to doing social work with the SC Department of Social Services. Over the years he advanced to heading child abuse investigations for Berkeley County S.C. He later moved on to working with special needs children in the State's custody.

After ten years with social services, H.L. returned to his love of building and became a licensed residential contractor. For twenty years he built custom homes and did high end renovations. He recently retired, but still happily putzes around the neighborhood as a handyman, as well as exasperating Denise, and loving on his kids and grandchildren.

According to H.L. his crowning achievements in life are his marriage and three daughters. Finding happiness in life by living a moral existence, and learning the lessons of humility, love and kindness are really the only things that matter to him. He believes all else is extraneous distraction.

"If you believe that Creation has an intelligent design,

And that Creation is the work of a Divine Entity,

And that all things are connected in the design,

Then there is no greater joy than to walk in the light of the Divine,

Regardless of which paths present themselves,

And which paths you chose to follow."

H.L. Sawyer

Preface:

It's Complicated Yet Simple

In most absurdity, there is a grain of truth. In most grains of truth there is absurdity. HL Sawyer

An epistemology is the theory of knowledge that separates justified beliefs from opinions.

When it comes to a belief in a Higher Power, there are many opinions because of the metaphysical nature of the subject matter.

The existence of a God, Creator, or any term you are comfortable with using inevitably requires a leap of faith. The very concept of a Divine initiator of Life is beyond our comprehension. The specifics of a Creator are beyond esoteric.

Even more daunting is the sheer volume and diversity of religious doctrine in the world today. While all, to some extent or another, share the belief that the underlying essence of Creation is love, interpretations of how to live vary widely. From the Buddhist path to Enlightenment to the Christian rebirth in Christ as holding the keys to Heaven, life's guidebooks can be vastly different.

Another thing religious doctrine all have in common is that they are primarily based on ancient teachings without any significant updates. While the New Testament could be considered the Bible 2.0, that was the last update…. some 2,000 years ago.

Much has changed in 2,000 years since the arrival of Christianity and 2500 years since Buddhism came into belief. The same is true for Hinduism, Islam, Judaism, and many lesser-followed religious practices…most religious doctrines are ancient and without significant revision.

While there is really nothing new under the sun, what I offer is not a new religion per se but rather a new perspective on how to live one's life within the context of one's beliefs. That Creation and the Creator are good, that Life is inherently more positive than negative, and behind the light which emanates Creation is love.

My perspective overlays advances in quantum physics and in general science on the predominant religious belief systems of today. My work is not meant to be an aspersion or an endorsement of any system but rather a means to add clarity to one's preferred beliefs.

One's preferred belief system is a deeply personal belonging. Casting doubt on one's beliefs often evokes anger in the believer. This is not my intent. Instead, I believe that when doubt is cast on anything valid, the result should yield more certainty. Doubt is a path to deeper understanding.

To my readers, I am most grateful to you for taking the time to consider my conceptualizations. I am sure to many, much of what I say may ring true, I am equally sure to others, much may not. Regardless, I am hopeful you will find my words thought-provoking and helpful in your personal quests down life's paths.

Much has changed over the millennia. Our awareness of our physical world has grown exponentially. A lot has changed since Jesus walked the Earth in sandals. Jesus's parables never once mention quantum mechanics. He never had the luxury of Googling. Things were vastly different back in His time.

Breakthroughs in science, particularly the field of quantum mechanics, have wedded physics and religion as never before. My words are an attempt to update shared beliefs, in light of new discoveries. Discoveries that illuminate the paths leading to both confirmation and a deeper understanding of spiritual doctrine.

As a side note, authoring a traditional book is not an ideal format by which to attempt such an endeavor. By nature, reading is a linear process. Non-fictional works attempt to use words in the linear form of sentences to make logical arguments. Books are organized in distinct sections known as chapters and present quantifiable data both logically and sequentially.

Nothing in this work of mine, and/or the like-minded gleanings of others, is either quantifiable by data or linear. Spiritual matters do not exist within the logical confines of linear time and space.

Our existence as sentient beings, like the existence of our Creator, goes beyond time and space. The confirmation of spiritual beliefs can only be qualified and confirmed through analogy, parable, and deep-rooted instinctual beliefs, Spirituality is not linear and rarely manifests sequentially.

I offer this work as a manual to consider the belief that Awareness is the foundation of who you really are. That your Awareness is linked to a Divine Awareness of a Higher Power. By recognizing and using this conceptual connection, you can refine the quality of your beliefs, and improve your life and the lives of others.

THE RESULTS WILL BE SELF-EVIDENT.

What follows is a series of short vignettes on the nature of the quantum realm, the spiritual realm, and possible relationships between the two. It is by no means meant to be a steadfast theory to unify the two. It is rather an attempt to open one's eye to a new realm of possibilities...to examine the certainty of one's religiosity in the light of today's scientific advancements....to cast the light of doubt to enhance certainty and diminish falsehood in one's beliefs... to offer a new conceptual path to happiness and a closer relationship to all that is Divine.

While my words and thoughts may offend some who are steadfast in their beliefs, my intent is not incursive to any belief system. Instead, I hope to shed light on the realm of all possibilities that the quantum world now suggests.

"Any fool can make something complicated,

It takes a genius to make it simple" –Woody Guthrie

Chapter 1

A Brief History of Mankind

'They say time changes things, but you actually have to change them yourself.'

Andy Warhol

Mankind's evolution has been a long journey. From the first step of Homo habilis some 2 million years ago to Homo Erectus some 500,000 years ago, mankind's ancestry has had many branches. It has been a long climb up the evolutionary ladder.

Some 300,000 years ago, Homo Sapiens arrived. Homo Sapiens is the precursor of modern humans. It took Homo Sapiens around 250,000 years (give or take several thousand years) to develop the communication skill of language.

Some 12,000 years ago, the emergence of agriculture began to take shape. The nomadic hunter cultures began to give way to settlements. Settlements became towns, and towns became cities.

Some 3.500 years ago, written language was born in Mesopotamia, a.k.a. 'the cradle of civilization.' Advancements in the wheel, the weaving loom, and the use of irrigation were among the first technologies invented.

Some 2,500 years ago, the prominent religious teachings of today began to take shape. Two thousand-five hundred years later, the teachings have very much remained intact. The factual nature of the teachings is unaltered and rarely questioned.

About the time today's prominent religious teachings were founded, daily life was far different than today. Modest homes, built of stone, mud, and straw, included tables, a chair or two, wooden bowls, and an olive lamp for light. A few tools, such as a wooden spinning wheel, utensils, and a fire pit for cooking, were standard. It was a primitive, hardscrabble existence.

Occupations such as carpenters, blacksmiths, fishermen, masons, farmers, soldiers, and city officials grew. Civilization, as we know it, was in its infancy.

Women were not allowed to read and were relegated to making and caring for babies; the daily chores of maintaining a home and working in the fields would be a fair generalization. Literacy rates were meager.

At the time of Christ, at best, 10% of the populace could read. Most who could read were among the wealthiest class. History and knowledge were primarily shared as an oral tradition. Such were the origins from which Biblical knowledge was born.

A Eulogy to Cosmo

Fast forward to today, and it is shocking to see the changes that have occurred. From the standpoint of a chronological timeline, the last two thousand years were but a blip on the screen. The last 500 years but a millisecond. The last 200 years, but a nanosecond.

For anyone who walked the Earth at the time of Jesus, today's world would be unrecognizable. They could only conclude that today's world was the creation of an advanced alien race that had assumed a human form. They would stare in awe at a skyscraper and ask themselves, 'Am I in Heaven?'.

In contrast to the light-year improvements manifested in the physical world, human nature has followed a slower pace. In most parts of the world, women remain subservient. Hate is still manifested in wars. The only difference with war is the increased efficiency in which it destroys. With the omnipresence of knowledge available to nearly all and enough resources to sustain all, one would think the heart of human nature would have grown kinder. A world where primal instincts for self-preservation become tempered by the moral imperative to provide for the common good.

One would think that human nature would have evolved to recognize the equality of men and women, the futility of war, and, in general, more manifestations of our higher natures and reduced manifestations driven by our lesser natures. While the modes of transportation have advanced from that of the chariot to that of a supersonic jet, the person who guides the reins remains much the same.

So why haven't improvements in human nature kept pace? Albeit it can be argued that human nature has become somewhat advanced, it has nowhere near approached the advancements technology has brought to the physical landscape. [OBJ]

To further address this question, examining the evolution of religious doctrine would be a logical starting point. Religious doctrine is the guidebook for living a moral existence. Religious doctrine defines human nature and how best to manifest one's actions toward the good of humanity and Creation.

To begin, let us look at the evolution of Christianity. Two thousand years ago, the doctrine of Christianity was disseminated orally. In fact, the life of Jesus was not even recorded on papyrus until a generation later. Jesus spoke in the Aramaic language. Initially, the text was written in Greek by unnamed authors. It was written without any first-hand accounts. Yet the vast majority of today's Christians assume the Gospels are the verbatim words of Jesus and that the Gospels are a purely factual biographical account without error or hyperbole. They also believe that the Gospels are the singular path to a positive afterlife.

With all due respect to my evangelical friends, I find this astounding. When a story is passed orally from one person to another, the story inevitably changes. While the basic premise remains the same, many details are altered. Retold enough times, even the basic premise can change. When the basis of the story is a tale of exquisite proportion, the deeds of the hero often become exaggerated as well.

While the parables of Jesus are incredibly beautiful, and their lessons withstand the test of time, their origins are uncertain.

When we review the factual history of the Gospels of Jesus, we ascertain the following:

1. Jesus lived in an era when life was primitive, and most people were illiterate

2. The teachings and the life events of Jesus were largely recorded via oral traditions

3. The Gospels were written a generation later without the benefit of any first-hand accounts.

4. The Gospels were originally written in Greek and then transposed to Latin around 400 A.D.

5. The Gospels were transcribed by anonymous authors.

6. The Gospels were not translated into other European languages until much later; The English translation was in 1382, the Spanish translation was in 1569, and the Italian translation was in 1607.

7. Even when translated into local languages, literacy rates remained extremely low, and memorization of scripture was the primary means of learning. [OBJ]

The second-hand accounts of the Gospels are not unique to religious doctrine. Instead, the accounts of most central religious doctrines of the world follow a similar path. It is fair to assume all religious doctrines are painted with hyperbole to some degree or another.

Technology has been advanced by people who possess the imagination and dare to challenge the status quo. Collaboration and diversity of opinion lead to technological advancement. Technological change alters normative behaviors. When change leads to improvements in everyday life, change is good. Positive changes are the engines of progress.

The advancement of human nature, likewise, can only move forward when we begin to challenge the very paradigm of our belief systems. While various branches have sprung within multiple religions, the variations are narrow. The branches are limbs from the same tree. Change is thus limited to the genre of the tree. Our belief systems remain segregated to the genre of their 'respective seed.'

What we often fail to acknowledge is the existence of 'other trees' within the same ecosystem. In Nature, forest trees have evolved to form cooperative, interdependent relationships. For example, the roots of different tree species often become entangled with each other. This provides all the trees with greater strength to protect them from storms. Trees share nutrients and information to defend against insects. Trees are interconnected by fungi that grow out of their root tips to form vast networks to transfer nutrients to areas where they are less abundant. We can learn a lot from trees and fungi.

All trees require the same essential nutrients: soil, air, sunlight, and water. Though each tree has its own optimum elixir, the basic nutrients are the same. And when intertwined, they grow stronger together.

Religious beliefs also require the same essential nutrients: knowledge, wisdom, humility, and love. Like species of trees, different religious doctrines have their own optimum elixir of the same basic nutrients.

When religious beliefs are intertwined, we grow stronger together. When religious beliefs are intolerant, they sap our strengths and resources.

Technology currently stands on the precipice of discoveries that will change not only how we live but also the paradigm of who and what we are. The field of quantum physics offers not only vast gains in a wide swath of technologies but insights into the basic foundations of our belief systems as well.

Quantum physics turns many of the notions of traditional physics on their head. Traditional physics basically follows a linear line of logical, intuitive explanations of outcomes. Quantum physics follows a path of explanations of outcomes based on seemingly illogical, counterintuitive multiple possibilities.

Traditional physics quantifies the physical world under the assumption that events occur uninfluenced by our observations. Quantum physics recognizes events that occur under the influence of our observations.

Quantum physics postulates that our beliefs exist as energy and thus can influence physical outcomes. It also proposes that internal and external realities are connected in a two-way relationship.

Quantum physics casts doubt on the certainty of all our core beliefs.

Much like in the forest, where nature connects all genres of trees for the benefit of all, quantum physics potentially offers insight into similar connections for the benefit of all humanity.

Much like the basic nutrients of trees, the basic nutrients of human nature are the same for all humanity. When our beliefs become entangled, we become stronger. When our beliefs are nurtured with knowledge, wisdom, humility, and love, our entire ecosystem gains positivity.

I believe quantum physics may soon quantify that knowledge, wisdom, humility, and love are the true purpose and path for all humanity to follow. Furthermore, it will quantify that in the quantum realm of possibilities, there is more than a single path to manifest our shared true purpose. Whatever afterlife is to follow is a continuation of the belief system each Being has manifested within the internal universes that exist within each of us.

What follows in this writing are my ramblings on the marriage of science and religion. An attempt to superimpose the pathways of the quantum world and science in-general, with the paths of our beliefs. To cast doubt in the pursuit of certainty.

Casting doubt on one's beliefs builds certainty in true beliefs.

What I hope to accomplish in my writing is how to better envision and thus connect our individual Beings as arbitrators between God and the physical realm in which we live. That living is not just a series of binary events but rather a realm of infinite possibilities. That living is a conversation between 'our Selves' and our Creator. That our beliefs and actions when guided by positivity, create positivity. In creating positivity, we act as the hands of God and are reflecting the image of our Creator. By reflecting the image of our Creator, we are fulfilling the ultimate purpose of Creation.

The basic building block of light is the photon. I hope that this work adds a photon of positive light to the world. And that my photon sparks other photons, thus better illuminating the path of knowledge, wisdom, humility, and love.

Chapter 2
Setting the Stage

The Logicality of Faith

"Faith is not believing in my own unshakeable belief. Faith is believing in an unshakeable God when everything in me trembles and shakes. "

Beth Moore

To produce correct and valid reasoning, one must consider all possibilities. In the physical realm, this is infinitely easier than the spiritual realm. In the physical realm, one can test a theory against all possibilities, and it can either be proven correct or incorrect. Theories, proven correct, become the laws of nature. A straightforward process. A binary process that can be built upon. A foundation grounded in logic and certainty.

In the spiritual realm, finding a 'foundation of certainty' is oxymoronic. It is simply not possible to attain definitive empirical results. The scientific method does not apply to spiritual beliefs. Logic in the spiritual realm is often suspended and replaced by the unverifiable.

The foundation of certainty in the spiritual world is faith.

Faith is an assumption based on evidence that falls short of absolute proof. Faith is used to 'fill in the blanks' in the light of uncertainty. Faith is like an ethereal glue to which to attach one's beliefs. Faith plus beliefs is the formula for the creation of all religions.

In the spiritual realm, there are no physical laws. Without physical laws, anything is possible. The spiritual realm is governed by faith and belief. 'Reality' in the spiritual world is in the eye of the beholder.

All religions/faiths begin at a starting point. On one side of the spectrum, we could start with Buddhism. Buddhism is a non-theistic abstract belief in Nothingness being at the heart of the Universe.

On the other end of the spectrum, we could start with Christianity. Christianity is a specific theistic belief that Christ was the Divine manifested in human form and giving oneself to His body is the singular means to salvation.

It can be inferred that Buddhism and Christianity are, in many respects, at the opposite poles of belief systems. Buddhism being 'the 0', and Christianity being 'the 1'. It can likewise be inferred that there is an infinite realm of possibilities between the two.

While Buddhism and Christianity are quite different, they do share similarities.

Both believe that compassion and love are the quintessential elements of life.

Both believe that misdeeds such as murder, stealing, lying, and sexual misconduct are contrary to their faiths.

In order to accept a religion/belief system, one must start somewhere.

Logic tells me that the starting point is a Creator. My mind is comfortable with the assumption that the ultimate beginning of the universe is a Creator. That said, the Creator is beyond all comprehension. Unlike my Buddhist friends, I am not concerned with the Nothingness prior to creation. Instead, I am more concerned with the order, beauty, the mechanics of how the universe works, and its intelligent design.

My second assumption is that God created us in His image. That image is the ability to create. The ability to live with love and compassion and thus create an internal universe at my core that mirrors the image of God.... which by His/Her nature is both compassionate and infinite.

Thus, my faith is simple.

1. The Creator is the proper focus of my beliefs.

2. Creation has an underlying intelligent design based on love and compassion.

3. I am created in God's image and have the ability to both create my own internal universe and positively influence the external world I exist in.

4. By creating my internal universe based on love and compassion, I am fulfilling my purpose in life and beyond.

These faiths are the assumptions upon which I develop my beliefs. They clearly fall somewhere in between the 0 and 1 of Buddhism and Christianity. I passionately believe they are the correct basis of who I am and what I am meant to be. They are every bit as valid as the beliefs of the devout Buddhist or devout Christian.

Perhaps I should add an addendum to my faith tenets....

5. All religious tenets are equally valid if they prove consistent with their assumed belief in a benign Creator or Natural force.

I am guessing here, but I get the feeling that some readers may especially disagree with my 5th tenet. Some will remain adamant that their religious beliefs are either superior or even the only true path; I would suggest such is not the case. I would humbly submit that such restriction is counterintuitive to the infinite nature of the Divine. I would further suggest, as we shall soon see, that science suggests such narrow thinking is likewise counterintuitive to the vast interconnectivity of Nature. Finally, I might offer the adage, 'When one is full of oneself, there is no room for others.'

It is perfectly ok to question a fundamental tenet of one's faith. If you have never looked at your faith from the point of view of others, you have no perspective. If you have never kept an open mind to another's view because it is upsetting to your faith, you are doing a disservice to your faith.

Faith is the basic assumptions upon which Beliefs are built

Beliefs and actions are the building blocks of who and what we really are

Divine Awareness

I think, therefore, I am

Rene Descartes

The mind does not generate Divine Awareness.

Divine Awareness is the thoughts of God. All knowledge is generated by the thoughts of God.

Awareness is the interplay of individual consciousness with Divine Awareness.

Awareness is received through the 'third eye.' The 'third eye' is attuned to the frequency of the Divine. Everyone has their own unique frequency of Awareness. Like an old radio dial, each frequency can be fine-tuned by the individual.

Divine Awareness is that faint voice within. The white noise of the mind. When one becomes submerged in the relativities of everyday life, one's frequency with the Divine can be diminished. The negative aspects in life act as clouds that block the positivity of the Divine. Positive aspects in life improve reception.

When one opens the third eye, one opens the mind to knowledge. Perception is gained through Awareness. One's feelings and actions gain positivity.

In the physical world, your beliefs and actions define who you are. Consciousness and Awareness comprise the 'Being' who you are. When you are 'Being 'aware,' your Being has the ability to attach attributes to all things properly... When you are 'Being aware',' you qualify all things with Divine light. The attributes of your Being move closer to the Divine. When you are' Being aware,' you get closer to the essence of all things, and your actions and feelings follow suit. Being aware gives you the ability to qualify your beliefs and take actions in accordance with the will of the Divine.

The third eye is simply the means to visualize and access Divine thought. It is not so much a function of vision as it is a function of listening. If we assume one's Being is created in the image of God, the third eye is the channel by which ones' Being communicates with ones' image of the Creator.

Divine Awareness is the mind of God. When you act in Awareness, you modify both your Being and the world toward the Divine. The light of the Divine thus benefits your internal universe and the external Universe.

Divine Awareness is simply the conscious act of learning to keep the 3rd eye open as you go about your daily tasks. To learn to filter sensory input through your inner Being. In doing so, you are not only influenced by the sensory input, but can influence the input. (as we shall see in 'The Observer Effect')

Let us use a simple example. Let us assume that you are feeling good about yourself. You access your Inner Being and begin a conversation with the Divine. Your thoughts turn to why you are feeling good about yourself. You recognize your life is good. You own a nice house. You have a good job. You have a beautiful and kind wife. Healthy children. Good neighbors. There is a lot of positivity in your life.

In the light of Divine Awareness, you further qualify your feelings. You begin to realize you are not feeling good about yourself at all! You are experiencing happiness. Feeling happiness is different from feeling good about yourself. Feeling good about yourself is really a function of your Being doing good. Doing good is making your house a nurturing home, doing your job to the benefit of others as well as yourself, and loving and appreciating your wife. Loving and putting in the effort to nurture your children. Helping your neighbors when they need your help. All these actions are achieved in concert with Divine Awareness.

Your thoughts cascade downward toward the essence of what 'good' is. Your Awareness deepened your understanding of what 'feeling good' really is. You recognize that feeling good is achieved by doing good. Your definition of feeling good about yourself was misplaced. What you were feeling was happiness, a causal effect of doing good. Happiness will only last if your actions reflect good intentions.

The difference outlined here may seem a bit trite, but it is genuinely not. Feeling happy and feeling good are very different things. Digging deeper, you recognize you cannot 'do happy'; you can only 'do good.' To be happy you must do good. You conclude that doing good is the ultimate precedent of happiness. Doing good is the true path to happiness.

Accessing Awareness is more than prayer; it is a conversation.

Cosmic Entanglement

Does the flap of a butterfly's wing in Brazil set off a tornado in Texas?

Edward Lorenz

Quantum physics is a real epiphany. The theory of quantum entanglement is a proven science. The theory states that when two particles, such as photons or electrons, become entangled, they remain connected even when separated by vast distances of space. They can communicate instantaneously over light years of space. Much of quantum physics flies far from the traditional laws of physics and violates the rules of space and time.

Quantum entanglements defy space and time as well as logic. How can particles influence each other instantaneously over light years of space?

But quantum entanglement is a real principle that has been proven time and again. There is a growing consensus amongst physicists that entanglement is indeed real, and space/time are fabrication of our making. Its implications and applications are vast.

Quantum entanglement leads me to another question.

Could there exist a Cosmic Entity that connects us

to the universe and beyond? An energy that exists beyond our perceptions and that defies linear logic. A direct frequency to the Divine, whose only encumbrance is the density of the physical world, relegating the Divine to a faint voice within. As in quantum physics, a cosmic entanglement, not between photons but rather Awarenesses, that can communicate over infinite distance, instantaneously.

The Human Entanglement

'What's the frequency, Kenneth?' R.E.M

Awareness is the entanglement between consciousness and the Divine.

Consciousness cannot be explained purely as a matter of brain function.

Science offers us no viable explanation. Science cannot measure consciousness. You cannot look inside the brain and quantify thoughts, feelings, or beliefs because consciousness does not exist in space and time. Yet, it exists and requires energy.

Consciousness and Awareness are partners in a quantum entanglement.

Awareness is the sum of our mind/body experiences (consciousness) when filtered through the prism of Divine Awareness.

Awareness on the macro level are the thoughts of 'God'.... or any name you wish to assign to the casual architect of the Universe. Using the term 'Divine Awareness' to represent the Creator offers us an opportunity to explore 'God' both beyond preconceived restraints of religious dogma as well as in tandem with the precepts of one's belief system.

On a micro level, Awareness is the DNA of God…the microchip seeded within all things. The connection that is shared by all things.

Everyone and all things have a unique frequency (ability) to connect with Divine Awareness.

While a sedentary object like a rock has a very faint and stable frequency, humans have a much higher and more volatile frequency. The human frequency can grow stronger or diminish depending on how attached or removed we become to the physical world.

Awareness is that slight white noise you hear in your mind…the 3rd eye. The voice of intuition, creativity, clairvoyance, and wisdom. Consciousness/Awareness is who you are!

I love blue skies

I've looked at love from both sides now,

From give and take and still somehow,

It's love's illusions, I recall.

I really don't know love at all

Joni Mitchell

Is the sky blue? Surprisingly, the answer is no. The sky's most predominant color is violet. However, due to shortcomings in the cone cells of the human eye, we interpret it as blue.

So, when one observes the sky is blue, one is not correct. We simply see the sky as blue due to perceptual limitations. The physical reality is the sky is violet.

I love blue skies; This is a totally accurate observation. While the physical observation that the sky is blue can be proven false. One's feelings cannot be proven or disproven. Because feelings do not exist in space and time, they cannot be quantified. Even when manifested in the physical world, feelings cannot be measured and thus not quantified.

Love is a feeling, an attachment, an affection, a need, and a desire.

Love does not occupy physical space, yet it exists. It exists in our consciousness. Consciousness organizes brain activity. Brain activity requires energy. Within consciousness, feelings, such as love, likewise require energy. Love is an energy every bit as real as any quantifiable energy of the physical world.

The energy of love is every bit as real as the energy from the sun that paints the sky violet.

Divine Awareness is where love emanates. And just like our eyes have limitations and misinterpret the color of the sky, limitations in our Awareness cause us to misinterpret love.

In addition to misinterpreting the color of the sky, some days, clouds block the entirety of the sky. This, too, happens with Divine Awareness. Clouds of hate, anger, jealousy, and lust often block love's essence in the physical realm. Like our cone cells limit the essence of the sky's color, negative emotions limit the essence of Divine love.

The more we open our Awareness to that of the Divine, the more the clouds of negativity dissipate in our lives.

Awesomeness

'Great things are done by a series of small things brought together.'

Vincent Van Gogh

The world is both wondrous and harsh. The intricacies of Existence are mind-boggling.

It is awesome for life to even exist. Without proper proportions of sunlight, life cannot exist. Without water, life cannot exist. Without an ozone layer, life cannot exist. Without the proper proportions of oxygen, carbon, nitrogen, and hydrogen, life cannot exist. I would guess there are thousands of scenarios where a slight change of circumstance could end life as we know it. Yet here we are.

Life exists on a razor-thin edge, and it is awesome that we even exist.

One cannot overstate the magnificence of Creation. It is boundless and beautiful. Sheer perfection is everywhere. A sunrise, the rhythm of the tides, the bloom of a flower, the birth of a child.

On the other hand, life can be harsh. Anger, violence, and hate are all part of the human condition. The world is full of pride, greed, lust, envy, gluttony, wrath, and sloth…the seven deadly sins of Roman Catholic theology. How can one justify a benevolent

Creator who allows such pain to exist?

The answer is simple. Evolution. We are born into this world to evolve. To evolve not only physically but spiritually as well. Without hate, one would not know love. No pain, no joy.

Traditional physics teaches us time and space are relative to the motion of the observer and the observed object. Beliefs are likewise relative in our physical world.

Beyond the physical realm, it is simply counterintuitive to believe that in the light of a loving Almighty God, negativity could exist. What possible purpose would hatred fulfill? I speculate that the negative aspects that one carries to the afterlife are simply qualifiers for 'one's seat' relative to the light of the Divine. The more positivity, the better 'the seat.' The more aware, the closer to Divine Awareness.

Negatives are all creations of the physical world so we can understand the positives of a higher realm

Put a slightly different way, just as Einstein's theories of relativity prove that time is relative to one's physical frame of reference, so too are human emotions relative to one's Awareness. Einstein recognized the synchronicity of the physical and spiritual, when he postulated, "All religion, arts, and sciences are the branches of the same tree."

Thus, the difference between the wondrous and the harsh is that the wondrous has its roots in Divine Awareness, and the harsh has its roots in the physical world. The harsh exists so we can experience the wondrous. When one experiences hate, anger, and pain, these emotions act as clouds that block the light of Divine Awareness.

It is a higher purpose of living to learn to qualify negativity as subservient to positivity. To recognize that love exists on a higher plane than hate.

The Leap of Faith

'The fact of quantum entanglement is this. If one logically inexplicable thing is known to exist, then this permits the existence of all logically inexplicable things.'

Brian McGreevy

Science can measure and explain much in our perceived physical realm. But there is much in our physical realm that cannot be explained. The scientific definition of who and what a human being is, falls far short of an explanation of the causal root of the human Being. The how and why we exist has yet, not even been broached by science.

Religion, until now, has been the exclusive venue for defining the who, what, how, and why of existence. The causal roots of religion are the inscribed teachings of wise individuals who lived long ago. Their designations range from wise men to prophets of God, to God himself manifested as a man. Their teachings are delivered through the written word and organized into a body of knowledge known as doctrines. Religious doctrine is in part proven by parables and analogies that connect the physical world to a higher Being or force that has ultimate control both in the physical realm and what lies beyond. Some religious doctrine is a further extension of the beliefs gleaned through the words of their founders by those that followed.

The premise of all religious doctrine requires a leap of faith to subscribe to their beliefs.

Followers of religious doctrines accept the doctrines based on feelings that the beliefs ring true to their causal root. That causal root is their Being (soul). The path to the confirmation of the doctrine is, in large part, influenced by the origins of their physical environment as well as the paths followed in life.

Until now, there has been little (if any) overlap between science and religion. Concepts such as entanglement born from quantum theory are beginning to offer a bridge between the physical and the spiritual. They offer vast innovative technologies which may soon provide insights into the causal root of Being.

An underlying principle of quantum theory is that of a monistic universe. A universe that weds consciousness to matter.

An example of this was recently produced by Google's Sycamore quantum computer, which generated what scientists believe is an artificial wormhole.

Although the experiment was limited in scope, it nonetheless proved a process of communication (and perhaps travel) is possible beyond time and space.

The implications of this breakthrough are vast. One day, it may move us much closer to a scientific link to the Creator and creation.

Until such a time that a linkage is discovered, we are relegated to relying on religious doctrines and the intuitive beliefs they inspire. While religious doctrine and spiritual beliefs remain our primary guide to finding one's purpose and direction, quantum physics may soon offer insight into the mind of Creation.

At this juncture in time, my interpretation of the mechanisms of Divine Awareness are more attuned to spirituality than science. While quantum physics, psychology and biology have all made discoveries that imply a connected universe, nothing yet is near to a definitive 'unified theory' of the physical to the spiritual.

The same holds true in religion and spirituality. The only true connection between the physical and the spiritual realms are the intuitive perceptions of our inner Being. Connecting the physical to the spiritual thus requires a leap of faith. A leap of faith to conceptualize deep-seated internal beliefs as truth. Faith is the internal belief system that connects the physical world to the spiritual realm.

But I do believe when one overlays aspects of today's science onto one's belief system, a certain amount of clarity and certainty can now be achieved. The distance of the 'leap' becomes shorter, and the path clearer. The path to Divine Awareness is a dynamic process, ever-evolving, not unlike the paths of scientific discovery.

Divine Awareness requires a leap of faith as a path to clarity of one's beliefs. It is a complement to one's beliefs.

Divine Awareness is a path to a deeper personal relationship with a Higher Power.

Who am I?

'In the end, you don't so much find yourself, as you find someone who knows who you are.'

Robert Brault

I own a truck. I love my truck. My truck transports me from point A to point B. My truck needs fuel and maintenance to run. I let my truck get full of crap. I occasionally clean it up. I am not a very tidy person. My truck is, in some ways, an extension of my personality.

I have a mind/body. It transports me from point A to point B. My mind/body needs fuel and maintenance to run. I let my thoughts get filled with clutter.

I occasionally reconsider my thoughts and beliefs and reevaluate things. My mind/body is an extension of my Being.

My mind/body changes over time. About every seven years, nearly all the cells in my mind/body regenerate. Very subtly I morph into a different configuration. I was once a baby, a child, a teen, a young man, a middle-aged man, and now an old man.

It is only my inner Being that has remained a constant. It is my inner Being who has witnessed who I was, am, and am yet to be.

I am aware of the changes in my mind/body and aware of the realities of my past and present involvements, as well as speculations on what the future holds in store.

AWARENESS is who I am. AWARENESS is who you are!

Chapter 3
Being Aware

Living in Awareness

'Nothing in life is to be feared; it is only to be understood. Now is the time to understand more so we can fear less.'

Marie Curie

Living in Awareness is quite simple. It requires little effort. No mental gymnastics is necessary. No special breathing techniques, chants, or deep meditation need to be mastered. While meditation amplifies one's frequency, there are simpler ways to gain a similar result.

Living in Awareness is simply a commitment to reprioritize one's thinking.

As we go about our daily lives, we do so with the priorities of the physical world, front and center. That need not be changed. All that needs to be done is to filter your activities through your eye of Awareness Much like when you take a selfie on your cell phone camera. Today's cameras automatically filter out imperfections such as blemishes, poor background lighting if you blink, etc. Turning on your Awareness helps you filter out similar imperfections.

Awareness seeks positivity in situations and things.

All you must do is tell your conscious mind to turn on your Awareness filter.

It is as simple as changing your phone settings.

Your Awareness will automatically turn on, and all your actions, interactions, feelings, and thoughts will be filtered through a lens of positivity.

Changes in your perceptions and attitudes will be nearly indiscernible at first. But eventually, as you learn to master the use of your Awareness filter, the changes will become more apparent.

There are four stages in learning to use your Awareness (and learning in general)

1. Unconscious incompetence, where you are clueless.

2. Conscious incompetence, where you recognize your lack of ability.

3. Conscious competence, where if you try, you gain an ability

4. Unconscious competence, where your ability has become rote.

Let us say, for example, your child is ill. It requires much of your time to provide care. Your child is cranky and a handful to control. You are missing time from work. Other life commitments must be postponed or simply canceled. You are feeling frustrated and even angry at the world. (unconscious incompetence)

Now, turn on your Awareness filter, and things change. First, you reconfirm that your child's health is the highest priority, and the other priorities can either be postponed or, in many cases, really do not matter. You gain perspective. (conscious incompetence)

You begin to view your child's illness as an opportunity. An opportunity to bond. An opportunity to perform a selfless act of kindness. You recognize that you are dealing with 'clouds,' negativities caused by the illness. Your frustrations diminish, and your ability to empathize increases. (conscious competence)

Hopefully, the outcome of the illness is a good one, and your child's health is restored. Even in the event of a bad outcome or tragic one, you will eventually take solace in knowing you did everything you possibly could. (unconscious competence)

Awareness is not a cure-all for what life throws at you, but it improves perspectives, perceptions, and outcomes.

I remember when my dad passed away. For several nights, I slept in a chair at his bedside in the hospital. I remember how awful it was, trying to rest in a chair and listening to my dad slip through death's door.

In hindsight, I would pay a million dollars to have that moment in time returned to me. Just to see my dad again, and feel the deep connection I shared with him in

life. I took solace in knowing I was there for him, and I acted appropriately. I shared his pain and gave him all I could. I remain grateful I was awarded the opportunities of that moment.

Living in Awareness requires little effort. It is the conscious act of manifesting the Divine into the moments of living. Once learned, it becomes an autonomic act.

Awareness Connects All Things

'Invisible threads are the strongest ties.'

Friedrich Nietzsche

Sentience is the ability to experience feelings and sensations. Sentience is not limited to humankind alone.

In 1973, botanist researcher Dorothy Retallack made an interesting discovery. She discovered that despite not having a central nervous system to feel pain (as we feel pain), plants can experience sensations.

Ms Rellack discovered plants react to music. When exposed to easy-listening music, the plants grew toward the speakers. When exposed to rock music, the plants' growth was stunted.

Thus, plants prefer Willie Nelson's "Always on My Mind" as opposed to Ozzy Osbourne's 'Crazy Train'.

How much a plant can feel is not fully understood. But plants can clearly experience sensations and are thus sentient.

In other studies, plants have displayed similar abilities of sentience. A University of Missouri study found when corn plants were played a recording of caterpillars chewing on leaves, the plants emitted an anti-caterpillar chemical to protect their leaves.

Flowering plants likewise respond to the sounds emitted by their pollinators and will enhance the sweetness of their nectar to attract them. They are cognizant of their surroundings.

Insects likewise display sentience. Bees have demonstrated the ability to facial recognition of their hive mates as well as learn complex tasks through observation. Ants have the ability to rescue nest mates buried beneath rubble. They can make tools.

Flies, mosquitoes, termites, and butterflies all show substantial evidence they experience pain. Although they have a central nervous system, it is far less complex than that of animals. Thus, how they experience pain is far less complex. If an insect can experience pain, it can equally experience joy. Insects are more than mindless automatons.

Fish are sentient. Birds are sentient. And all the animal kingdom is sentient as well.

We live in a world of living, suffering, and joyful beings. We are all creatures of Divine origin. Every living being has its own respective frequency of sentience, consciousness, and Awareness.

There is a world within our world A world of sentient perception and Awareness up and down the evolutionary ladder.

A symphony of Awareness frequencies undetectable to

human senses.

All life is sentient to some degree or another

All life possesses some degree of Self-Awareness.

All life possesses some degree of Divine Awareness.

Within our physical world, vast frequencies of energy exist that are beyond our perceptions, beyond our abilities to quantify, beyond our knowledge, and even beyond our imagination to envision their existence.

Emmanuel Kant theorized a noumenal world. A realm involving the essence as opposed to attributes. A world of things as they really are. Using Kant's definition:

Consciousness is a collection of mental attributes: thoughts, feelings, and beliefs.

When Consciousness is filtered through Awareness the essence of what all living things are, becomes clearer.

Love and Hate

'Hate is louder than love, but love is stronger than hate.'

Steve Harvey

Love is a central premise of Divine essence. To understand the parameters of love, one must first understand the parameters of hate.

Both love and hate are powerful emotions Love creates. Hate destroys.

Hate is a passionate dislike of someone or something. Hate manifests itself as anger and violence. At its highest degree of manifestation, its result is complete destruction. Nothing is left of its passionate dislike. With nothing left, hate dissipates.

Love is a passionate like of someone or something. Love manifests itself as pleasure and kindness. At its highest degree of manifestation, its result is a new creation. Love adds, hate detracts.

Thus, in terms of the result, hate destroys and then dissipates. Love creates and grows. At its essence, hate burns out; love burns brighter. Hate darkens light; love illuminates light.

The superior nature of love can easily be demonstrated. I do not believe anyone could deny that the birth of a newborn child brings an overwhelming sense of joy and awe. A sense of love and connectivity between parents and child and Creation in general. To this day, when I hear the old Stevie Wonder song, "Isn't She Lovely," I am immediately connected to Divine Awareness. The song is a beautiful tribute to the birth of a child. It transports me back to the birth of my girls. The sense of joy and awe returns to me every time I hear it.

Hate, on the other hand, has zero connection to anything Divine. It is purely a primal instinct rooted in the physical world. The next time you become hateful, look inside yourself. Look to see if your hate is shared by your divine self. I defy you to feel or make even the slightest connection between your hatred and the God that dwells within you. Perhaps you can make a false equivalence, but you are only fooling yourself. Connecting the Divine to your hatred is impossible.

Positivity is stronger than negativity.. Love is stronger than hate.

It all adds up

Those who are not shocked when they first come across quantum theory cannot possibly understand it...Neils Bohr

Time to once again revisit quantum physics, or quantum mechanics, to be more precise.

Quantum mechanics now stands on the cusp of revolutionizing how computers compute. As discussed, in quantum physics, two objects can interact simultaneously over vast distances of space. It is a proven fact that flies in the face of physics and logic...simultaneously.

A soon-to-be real-life application of this principle is quantum computing. Quantum computing makes use of subatomic particles to store information. Quantum computing uses qubits to store information instead of the traditional 0s and 1s. Qubits recognize the concept that matter can exist in entanglements and superpositions beyond 0 and 1. Qubits recognize that information can be BOTH 0 and 1 simultaneously. Qubits can exist in multiple states simultaneously, allowing computations to occur in parallel, making quantum computing faster as well as able to solve problems beyond the capabilities of traditional computing, To Be AND Not Be simultaneously is the power of quantum computing. It is confusing but mind-blowing.

What this means is that computing will now do computations

traditional computing could not dream of both in terms of interpretation and speed. Quantum computing is predicted to be literally, hundreds of millions times faster and more efficient than today's computing. The gains in a whole swath of technologies will be transformative.

Overall, quantum computing is still in its infancy, but as we all know, technology grows geometrically. It will not be long until quantum computing yields the unimaginable, imaginable.

So, if we were to make an inference that the mechanisms of quantum computing could be similar to the mechanisms of Divine thought, would that be completely off base?

Within our conceptual visions of the Creator, would it not be possible for Divine Awareness to communicate simultaneously without the limitations of the rules of space and time?

Do we not believe the Creator can manifest any and all possibilities instantaneously?

Could quantum computing, in some ways, mirror the language of the Creator?

Quantum mechanics demonstrates communications can occur in the physical world outside the parameters of space and time.

Thus, it is more feasible than not to assume our

Awareness likewise has the ability to communicate with another Awareness outside the parameters of space and time.

Just as quantum computing has developed practical benefits beyond traditional computing, developing your frequency with Divine Awareness can likewise spawn practical benefits.

The Observer Effect

'Separation of the observer from the phenomenon to be observed is no longer possible.' Werner Heisenberg

The famed 'double slit' experiment was first performed in 1801 by Thomas Young. In the experiment, two slits are cut in a screen, and waves of light are shot through the openings onto another screen. When the waves are projected on a second screen behind the slotted screen, they are demonstrated to behave as both waves and particles.

Now, this is where it gets interesting. More recent variations of the double-slit experiment have used highly developed instruments to observe the paths of the electrons. What they found is that the act of the instrument observing the electron paths CHANGED the electron paths.

While the prospect of human observation altering the paths of the electrons has not been proven, the concept is a logical extension.

On the human level, many studies have demonstrated the Observer Effect.

For example, when nutritionists study the eating habits of study groups, the groups tended to eat better than when they were not being observed.

Worker productivity improved when management made changes in working conditions. Some changes were meant to improve productivity, and some to reduce productivity. But regardless of the changes, worker productivity improved while management was actively observing.

When you click 'the on setting' in your consciousness to open your Awareness frequency to Divine Awareness, you are enabling divine wisdom to influence your behaviors.

Opening your Awareness to Divine Awareness opens the doors to the Observer Effect

When actions occur in the light of Divine Awareness, the quality of your actions/outcomes naturally improves.

Biocentrism

'Nothing is good or bad, but thinking makes it so.'

William Shakespeare

Dr. Robert Lanza is a renowned scientist and doctor specializing in cell regeneration. He has authored many books on a theory he labeled Biocentrism.

Lanza takes the Observer Effect and the mechanics of the quantum world many steps further. Lanza speculates reality is not only confirmed by our thoughts but is, in fact, created by our thought processes. In the biocentric universe, it is life and biology that are the centerpieces and in fact, the causal influence behind being, our universe, and reality. Without our conscious Awareness of the universe, the universe does not exist. The essence of all matter is the creation of our consciousness.

Most scientists dismiss Lanza's work, which places biology over physics as the governing law of science. They claim his theories are unprovable. However, since science has no plausible explanation for what exactly consciousness is, it is hard to get one's head around an entirely consciousness-based cosmology.

Regardless, Lanza's works are thought-provoking and, to many (me included), quite brilliant.

Religion

Imagine there's no countries. It isn't hard to do

Nothing to kill or die for, And no religion, too

John Lennon

Organized religion: Where does one begin? Such a vast and divergent topic. Christianity, Judaism, Islam, Buddhism, Hinduism, Taoism to name a few.

I am not a theologian. I do know a bit more about Judeo-Christian belief structures and do live in a predominantly Christian country. I will thus spend more time for the point of my treatise on said values.

Through written words, religions are guidebooks for living a life that leads to a path to a pleasant afterlife. Religious doctrine likewise establishes rules for moral behaviors and is the foundation of codified laws. Religions are a means to establish and maintain social order.

In past generations, going back to Biblical times, literacy rates were much lower than they are today. Memorization of Scripture and verse, as well as learning of oral traditions, was a foundation of education for illiterate populations, Strict adhesion to literal interpretations was mandatory. Perceived violations were dealt with harshly.

A Eulogy to Cosmo

Some 300 years after the original New Testament was written, the premise of 'original sin' was added to doctrine. Original sin stresses that humankind is inherently tainted and has a proclivity for sinful conduct, further adding credence for the church to enforce moral order.

In the Middle Ages, Christianity was particularly harsh. While the most powerful European countries were not theocracies, the Catholic Church yielded great power. Both religious services and Biblical texts were in Latin. Though parish priests often were synonymous with corruptive behaviors, their knowledge of Scripture held them in high esteem and power. The Church's hold on society was ironclad, for it was the priests and not the kings who held the keys to eternal salvation or eternal damnation.

Beyond the Middle Ages and into the Renaissance, the Church remained a predominant force. The Church viewed science as complimentary as both were fields of study that ultimately drew attention to God and his creation; however, when science followed a contrary path to the written word, the honeymoon ended.

When Copernicus first proposed a heliocentric universe, the Catholic church accepted his findings, though they reneged their position and joined the Protestant church in calling his work heretical and contrary to scripture. Copernicus soon died after the publication of his work in 1543 and was declared a heretic posthumously.

When Galileo published his works supporting heliocentric theory, he too was labeled a heretic by the Roman Inquisition. While many heretics were burned at the stake, Galileo got off relatively easily. After he was forced to renounce his works, he was given a life sentence to house arrest.

I make mention of the above only to provide a sliver of background information. Most religions, at some time or another, have demonstrated levels of hate and intolerance when confronted with issues or events that go contrary to their beliefs. I think a case could be made that both Christianity and Islam have at times been particularly brutal. But that is beyond the scope of this writing.

Religions are 'how to' guidebooks on how to lead a life that will take you to an afterlife with a favorable outcome.

Religions throughout history have codified moral behaviors.

Religions throughout history have been a means of social control and have been intolerant of anything deemed contrary to their teachings.

Intolerance is contrary to Divine Awareness;

therefore, religion can be manifested improperly.

Christianity, to its followers, is the four Gospels of Jesus Christ. Jesus is recognized as the Son of God and thus Divine. A divine entity who sacrificed his life for the benefit of humankind. His sacrifice offers a means for people to be absolved from their sins and find eternal salvation through the declaration of Christ as one's personal savior.

Aside from Christianity, no other major religion presents its prophets as being Divine. In Judaism and Islam, the lives of prophets are used to teach belief systems and a path to an Afterlife. Christianity, Judaism, and Islam all share an overlap of their prophets. Though not Divine, the prophets are believed to have had a direct conversation with the Divine. Thus, their teachings are Divine inspired.

In Judaism, although there are no uniform teachings of an afterlife, there is a concept of Heaven. Heaven is open to righteous people of any faith whose actions on Earth warrant acceptance. Judaism does not recognize the concept of Hell. Hell is not entirely a physical place; rather it can be compared to a feeling of intense shame. A shadowy realm of existence,

Islam offers a paradise to those who follow Islamic duties in life. There is a hell for those who do not. Along with good deeds such as helping the poor, strict adherence to Sharia law is required. There is some leeway that believers of other faiths can enter their Paradise if they truly accept Allah in their final days.

In Christianity, good deeds are important, but a place in eternal Heaven or Hell ultimately rests in accepting Jesus as personal Savior. Only believers in Christ need to apply. Allegiance to Jesus overrides all actions. All misdeeds are wiped off the slate when one is reborn 'in the body of Jesus'.

In Hinduism, the laws of karma prevail, and reincarnation is the general rule. It is possible to escape the cycle of karma and achieve a higher plane through loving devotion, knowledge through meditation, and acknowledgment that self-hood is an illusion. Hindus have multiple deities, neither male nor female, but both. In Hinduism, Divinity and Nature are intertwined. Krishna is the primary God of Creation. They believe in multiple levels of 'heaven.'

Buddhists do not worship any gods or people, although the Buddha and others are revered as god-like for the level of spirituality they achieved. Buddhists believe in ridding oneself of human desire and the exercise of personal restraint.

Buddhism believes everything must come from something; thus, a Creator is not possible. Nothing is eternal. Mastering the concept of Nothingness is an underlying premise. Like in Hinduism, through meditation and personal enlightenment, the cycle of reincarnation can be broken, and Nirvana achieved. Nirvana is a place where there is no essence or selfhood. An eternal home of Nothingness,

Christianity, Islam, and Judaism all offer a continuation of a Selfhood afterlife based on varying degrees of deeds and faith in a Deity.

Hinduism and Buddhism, on the other hand, believe life is a cycle that can only be broken by relinquishment of Selfhood.

So, the question becomes which religion is correct. Is God exclusive to any one path? Does selfhood continue in the 'great beyond,' or is ridding oneself of selfhood the necessary path?

At its root, all religions are deeply held beliefs. One must ask if religion becomes a matter of 'Is the sky blue?' or 'I love blue skies!'.... Are physical words the truth, or are the emotions/beliefs they evoke the truth? As I have demonstrated, the physical is relative to our perceptions (the sky is violet), and emotions and beliefs (I love blue skies) cannot be proved or disproved. Could it be like, in the Biocentric universe, an afterlife is manifested by the beholder? Could the Hindu concept of Karma determine an afterlife be correct? Could it be that '0 and 1 are not our only choices?... that life is not a binary choice? Could it be that '0 and 1' and all possibilities in between exist?

A commonality with Western religions is that specific parameters of an Afterlife are predefined and binary by nature.

It is possible that in an Afterlife, there may be no specific predefined parameters, much like in quantum computing where 0 and 1 and all possibilities in between can exist simultaneously....

Religion by the Numbers

Just to add some perspective on religious beliefs let's do the numbers courtesy of Wikipedia.

Christianity	2.4 billion
Islam	1.9 billion
Secular/Agnostic/Atheist	1.2 billion
Hinduism	1.2 billion
Buddhism	5 billion

Far down the list is Judaism with a scant 15 million followers.

(And one of my favorites Bahai' at 5 million)

The population of the world in 2021 stood at around 7.9 billion.

Spirituality

I close my eyes in order to see

Paul Gauguin

Spirituality is an extremely broad term for people seeking meaning and purpose primarily from within one's Being. Thus, its tenets can be as diverse as individual breaths.

Additionally, the beliefs of indigenous tribal societies fall under the venue of spiritualism. Animism is the belief that all things in Nature possess a spirit that can be communicated with through various rituals. A primary Nature-centered God, surrounded by a pantheon of lesser gods and spirits, is a common belief structure.

Spirituality, on an individual level, is a belief system based on personal experience on what to think, and how to feel and live a moral existence. Additionally, spiritualists intuit what their vision of the afterlife looks like. Spiritualists look inward to find their faith. Spiritualists generally have a wider interpretation within the shared parameters of their fellow seekers. Spiritualists begin their quest from a position of doubt to find certainty.

Religion is based on the teachings of others, with more organized rituals and a standardized belief system for living a moral life and a path to a favorable outcome in the afterlife. Religious followers look outward to find their faith. Religions offer set parameters between their fellow parishioners. Religious followers begin their quest from a position of certainty and search to remove doubt.

Spiritualism and religion are not mutually exclusive of each other. They are both built on a similar foundation of understanding a positive meaning in life and establishing a relationship with a higher power. They both believe in moral principles and love as an underpinning of Creation. Adherents of spiritualism and religion follow the tenets of their respective callings, as well as seek a personal relationship with a Creator. (Aside from Atheists) Spiritualists, however, emphasize seeking a unique path, religious followers abide by a standardized path as prescribed by their scriptures.

Divine Awareness is compatible with both spiritualism and all religious doctrines.

Using one's Awareness is simply a tool to assess and grow one's spiritual path.

Is Jesus the ONLY way? A personal tale…

'When the eyes of the soul looking out meet the eyes of God looking in, Heaven has begun right here on this earth." A W Tozer

I have many Christian friends who are devout in their beliefs. They are good people. They are kind people. They are moral people. My friends talk the talk and walk the walk.

I was raised in a Jewish household. My father was very well-versed in the Old Testament. My mom was an agnostic theist. My parents were good people. They were kind and moral people. They also talked the talk and walked the walk.

My parents made me attend Hebrew school and have a Bar Mitzvah. After which, they let me decide if I wished to continue with organized religion. My answer was a resounding NO. Mom had won out. Along with my two brothers, we became a family that prayed to God at the dinner table but not at the temple.

In my later teens, I was first exposed to John 3:16 "For God so loved the world, that he gave his only Son, that whoever believes in him should not perish, but have eternal life."

So fair enough, I thought. Follow the precepts of Jesus, and you are going to Heaven. What I did not understand was conversion to Christianity and accepting Jesus as a personal savior was also necessary.

I was further informed of John 14:6 "No one comes through the Father except through me." So, I put it all together.

1. Accept and live the precepts of Jesus.

2. Convert to Christianity.

3. Accept Jesus as personal savior.

4. Jesus is the ONLY way to salvation.

Over the years, I have politely listened to a few friends and many Christian missionaries share 'God's good news' with me. At first, I listened intently, and gave a conversion to Christianity some serious thought. But over the years, and hearing the conversion pitch many times, I became angered. I began to view these people as patronizing bastards. Zealots who were so cocksure that their interpretation of Scripture was not only unquestionable but stood upon a pedestal of singular truth.

They were offering me salvation on the one hand and telling me the only other option was my eternal damnation. Since none of my ancestors were Christians, it was inferred they were all residents of Hell, or at least in a less-than-optimal existence. And what of the billions of good people who never were exposed to His gospels? Were they not allowed to enter Heaven? (I think the jury is still out on that one)

But since those days, I have taken the high road of forgiveness. For as Jesus said on the cross, "Forgive them for they do not know what they do" Luke 23:24. I realized they held a deep conviction and were trying to 'save' me but had not a clue how hateful and hurtful it felt to me.

I mention the above experience mostly for my Christian friends who have made it this far into my work. I realize some of what I say may be interpreted as offensive, again, not my intent. When I presented to Christians that perhaps John 14:6 could possibly be a misinterpretation of Jesus's words, my words fell on deaf ears.

When I propose that perhaps there are other paths to a Heavenly existence, this is never taken well by my devout Christian friends. They are usually very visibly upset. Questioning the certainty of this precept never goes well. They feel insulted. They fail to consider how insulting John 14:6 is to believers of other faiths.

From their perspective, I either accept Jesus as savior or face eternal damnation. From my perspective, I suggest that alternatives to a good afterlife are quite possible. I consider their position intolerant. They consider my words blasphemous.

As my Christian friends reject the notion of alternative doctrines to Christianity, I respectfully reject the notion of Christian exclusivity. Given we live in a realm of infinite possibilities, the Christian premise of a singular non-inclusive afterlife simply does not ring true.

Any religious tenet that is intolerant in nature is contrary to the nature of Divine Will

Christmas

'Christmas isn't a season, it's a feeling'

Edna Ferber

I live in America, where Christianity is the predominant religion. Every December, Christmas is omnipresent.

Christmas is the holiday marking the birth of Jesus Christ. It is a sacred religious event celebrating a new beginning. The beginning of the life of Jesus, the spiritual leader whose teachings form the basis of Christianity.

Prior to the arrival of Jesus, the winter solstice had long been a cause of celebration. It is the time when the Northern Hemisphere is tilted farthest away from the sun. It usually occurs on December 21st or the 22nd. When the axis of the northern hemisphere tilts 23.5 degrees away from the Sun, it marks the shortest daylight of the calendar days. The holiday celebrates the new beginning of spring. When darkness begins to recede, and light begins to grow.

In Pagan traditions, the winter solstice, also known as 'Yule,' is a festival that focuses on rebirth, transformation, and new beginnings. Many believe Stonehenge, a monument built in prehistoric times, was built to track the movements of the sun, moon, and stars. It was built as a 'temple' to celebrate the movements of the stars and moon. No doubt a place where Pagans worshiped their sun god. Today Druid ceremonies are still held at Stonehenge to mark the winter solstice.

The birth of Jesus is thus tied to the ancient traditions of hope and rebirth based on the renewal of light.

Christianity, more so than any religion, is the personification of the Creator of All as a human being. To Christians, Jesus is the manifestation of God in human form. Moreover, Christians believe Jesus's birth was unique. Jesus was conceived by a virgin mother from the power of the Holy Spirit of God. His divinity was thus not achieved but God-given.

Like the winter solstice celebrating the path of the sun, Christmas celebrates the path of the Son.... perhaps just a random irony of words.

Regardless of whether one follows the tenets of Paganism, Christianity, or any points in between, it matters little. Put another way, "It ain't the meat, but the motion."

Regardless of religious doctrine, what matters is that you manifest positivity.

Religious doctrines that manifest positivity are all paths to the same light.

As previously stated, a true manifestation in the physical

realm is that the sky is violet, and we are incapable of seeing it as anything other than blue. The true essence of Divine light is much the same and will only be revealed when our limitations are lifted.

A common speculation is that the Divine is manifested as a brilliant white light. White light is a combination of all colors in the light spectrum. I need to say no more.

Emptiness

'The kingdom of Heaven is closer than the brow above the eye, but mankind doesn't see it.'

Gautama Buddha

Emptiness is a central concept of Eastern religion/philosophy. Its premise is that what we perceive through our five senses, our perception of time and space, is not reality. That the essence of all things is not singular but is interconnected.

Safwan Zabalawi, a self-described 'happy citizen of the world,' explains it as follows:

Things are not really separate and fixed. Buddhism teaches that, in reality, they are always changing and interdependent.

The five senses only give us a 'surface identity.' We need the perceptions of the mind to understand the true nature of things and phenomena. The mind sees things made of information, not just matter. This information is not made of matter and has no material substance.

The field of information (consciousness) is empty of material substance. It is both a field of non-existence and existence.

To see the true nature of things, they must be observed through three projections.

1. How it changes through time

2. Through its interdependence with other things

3. Through its potentials

Zabalawi uses a tree as an example:

When we observe a tree, we identify it as a separate entity. We differentiate it by its leaves, color, size, etc. To see the tree's true nature, we must also see its roots, slowly expanding. We must see its roots absorbing moisture from the soil. We must see the air and sun's nutrients as part of the tree.

We must also see the tree's future potential. Viewed in winter, we must see its leaves grow and the fruit or flowers it will bear in the Spring.

The tree has no fixed identity of its own. It is interdependent with many things and is in a continuous state of change. All future manifestations of the tree are dependent on a plethora of factors.

Buddhism teaches that all things are interconnected and in a constant state of change.

In our minds, thoughts have neither form nor color as things in the physical world have. Yet thoughts exist. Like the physical world, thoughts change over time, are interdependent with other thoughts, and have infinite potential.

The mind thus exists neither in existence nor non-existence but between the two.

In Eastern religions, it can be generalized that true reality is the world of non-existence, a world where all is connected as One. Our minds are a medium in between two realms.

In Eastern religions, death is a merger into the connection of One. The dissolution of ego is the ultimate purpose of human existence. The farther one's ego is dissolved, the closer one approaches the ultimate paradise of existing in One. Reincarnation is the process that one must travel to achieve Oneness with creation.

Eastern religious doctrine teaches emptying one's Self from the illusions of the material realm is the ultimate path to happiness. In its void, wise people create their own Heaven and fools their own Hell.

Specter of the Gun

"Your mind is my mind, your thoughts are my thoughts." Mr. Spock.

Episode 6, Season 3, is one of my favorite episodes of the original Star Trek. The following synopsis is courtesy of Wikipedia.

The Federation starship Enterprise has been directed to make contact with a reclusive species known as the Melkotians. As they approach the Melkotian planet, they encounter a probe carrying a warning for them to stay away. Crew members hear the warning in their native languages, suggesting that the Melkotians are telepaths. Despite First Officer Spock's warnings about the formidableness of telepaths, Captain Kirk orders the ship to stay the course.

Once in orbit, Kirk, Spock, Chief Engineer Scott, Chief Medical Officer Dr McCoy, and Ensign Chekov transport to the surface.

They are met by a Melkotian emissary who declares that they have been condemned to death for trespassing.

The landing party then finds themselves in an abstract landscape that resembles an old Western town, though many of the buildings are only wooden facades. Furthermore, they find their phasers have been changed into six shooters, and they cannot contact the Enterprise.

Exploring the town, they find a newspaper dated October 26, 1881, the date of the infamous gunfight at the OK Corral. The townspeople believe the landing party are members of the Cowboys...Kirk is Ike Clanton, Scott is Billy Clinton, McCoy is Tom McLaury, Spook is Frank McLaury, and Chekov is Billy Claiborne.

The crew soon confronts the Earp brothers, Wyatt, Virgil, and Morgan, as well as their deputy, Doc Holliday, who are preparing to fight them at the appointed time

Knowing that in real history, the gunfight was fatal to most of the Cowboys, the crew tries to change their fates by getting the sheriff and townspeople to stop the fight. They attempt to negotiate with the Earps, but nothing works. However, when a barmaid, Sylvia, gets close to Chekov, a jealous Morgan Earp shoots him dead.

Spock remarks that the real Billy Claiborne had survived, suggesting that the day's events could be changed in other ways. To that end, Spock creates an improvised tranquilizer grenade to subdue the Earps before the shootout. But the gas fails to work,

The time of the shootout draws near. A defiant Kirk and landing party suddenly find themselves at the OK Corral with the Earps approaching.

Spock realizes from the failure of the grenade and the 'death' of Chekov that the world they are in does not conform to the laws of reality and persuades the others that if they are convinced of that, they cannot be harmed. Spock mind-melds with his team to imbue them with absolute conviction. Thus, when the Earps and Holliday open fire, their bullets pass harmlessly through.

Kirk beats Wyatt Earp in a fistfight and disarms him. When given the chance to kill him in revenge for Chekov, he instead throws his weapon away. The crew, including Chekov, next finds themselves back on the bridge of the Enterprise,

Due to Kirk's refusal to kill Wyatt, the Melkotians welcome the Enterprise to approach the planet and make contact.

I loved the original Star Trek. Though future configurations of the show each had their merits, it is hard to beat the stoic logic of Leonard Nimoy as Spock and the over-acting of William Shatner as Kirk. Spock, the emotionless one; Kirk, the over-emotional one,

In this episode the Mellkotians attempted to manifest the destiny of the Star Trek crew through their telepathic projections. Only through absolute belief did the crew overcome its prescribed fate.

Reality is sometimes neither clear nor obvious to the eye or mind

At its essence, reality is a projection that exists only when we believe in it

If we can convince ourselves something is not real, its rules no longer apply. But it takes a lot to transcend the rules. Maybe one day, science will invent a 'mind meld' apparatus that can hypnotize us to the point where we can transcend the negatives of physical reality. Something that can amplify faith to where we are all bulletproof to trauma, sadness, and pain. Something that requires faith not to be a blind leap but a certainty.

Perhaps in an Afterlife, we will be like the Melkotians. We will communicate telepathically. (how else to communicate if we do not have a mouth?) Perhaps one day, we will be advanced enough in our thought processes to erase negativity and embrace happiness. A place where faith can see through the blindfold without an iota of reservation.

Beam me up, Scotty!

Beyond a reasonable doubt

If we begin with certainties,

We shall end in doubts.

But if we begin with doubts,

And are patient; we shall end in certainties

Francis Bacon

In life, we have constructed a means to dispense justice. Justice is dispensed in light of the 'truth.' It is dispensed by courts of law. Laws being the recognized rules of behaviors and actions enforced by penalties when breached.

In life, all behaviors and actions are relative. For example, when an action results in a person's death, did the defendant kill or murder? Killing being there was some justification for his action in his intent, murder, having no justification for his intent. Intent either falls within or beyond the recognized rules of behavior.

It is beyond a reasonable doubt that the deceased is deceased. In fact, it is beyond an iota of doubt the person is deceased. No verdict will change this.

'Justice' can only go so far in life. Unless the defendant confesses his intent, the truth will never be fully served.

Confession is a concept central to many religions. In Catholicism, confession is a means to absolve oneself from 'the crime.' If one reveals one's intent and makes earthly amends, well, it helps. Absolution is the act whereby a priest acts as a surrogate for God, and grants God's mercy and is thus forgiven.

But total absolution of sin in Christianity requires more. One must be reborn in the Body of Jesus to be totally free of the 'crimes' of sin. One must confess Jesus to be one's personal savior to enter God's kingdom.

In life, justice operates at the standard of 'no reasonable doubt.' In Christianity and other religions, the afterlife operates under the standard of 'no iota of doubt One's faith must be certain.

In life, relativities exist in all feelings and behaviors. In death, the essence of all feelings and behaviors is revealed.

Only in the Divine light of essence can doubt be entirely lifted.

If we examine doubt in the light of Divine Awareness, we look at its positive nature. Doubt exists to stimulate, to question, to learn. Doubt is like a meadow between right and wrong, where we make decisions about what to believe and do.

Without doubt, there can be no certainty.

Whether one's beliefs take them down the path of Selfhood

(western religion) or the path of Selflessness (eastern religion), it is illogical to believe not an iota of doubt in one's beliefs can be achieved in a world of relativity. To do so, one would have had to achieve a Divine state and thus be Divine.

According to Christianity, only Jesus was Divine. According to all other predominant religions, there is no one who walked the Earth as a Divine entity.

It is perfectly acceptable to doubt one's core beliefs. In fact, doubt is the requisite of certainty.

Doubt is our guide to Certainty.

Questioning your beliefs through Divine Awareness is not a weakness, but rather builds strength of convictions.

Are you experienced?

When the power of love,

Overcomes the love of power,

The world will know peace

Jimi Hendrix

Letters are strung together to form words. Words represent things.

A-P-P-L-E is the word to represent an apple. When your eyes see the word 'apple,' your brain hears the word apple, and then you visualize an 'apple' in your mind.

But your mind is curious. It wants more data about an 'apple.' Words are strung together into sentences to elaborate. 'The apple is green'.... We now see its color.

The apple is smooth…. We now feel its texture. The apple is crisp…we now taste its taste. Based on your senses, the apple is manifested in your mind.

Words alone cannot describe an apple without the prerequisite of 'experiencing' an apple. When you were an illiterate baby your understanding of an apple began when you were first exposed to an apple.

Perhaps 'Baby You' first saw an apple on a tree, and your mommy held you up to the tree and put your finger on it and said 'apple.' That was your first experience with an apple. You visually perceived and touched the apple. 'The seed' of what an apple is was thus implanted in your brain.

'Infant You' continued to experience an apple as a food source. You tasted apple sauce and, at a little later age, bites of an apple. Your experience of what an apple is grew.

Emotions and feelings are much like an 'apple.' One can read about them, but the words are useless unless you have experienced them.

Let us return to the Blue-Sky analogy. Your mommy once pointed to objects and described them as blue. You thus learned the concept of blue. She then pointed at the sky and told you the sky was blue. This was your first experience with a blue sky.

Later in life, you learned to read. You learned about clouds, the sun, the ozone layer, and, eventually, electromagnetic energy. You stumbled upon deficits in the human eye and learned that the physical sky is NOT blue but violet.

Science has just undermined your experience of a Blue Sky.

But you are not buying it. You stare at the sky, but regardless of how long you stare, the sky's still blue. You look at the sky at various points of the day. At sunset, you see some violet, but learn that is only due to light reflection off clouds.

Your core belief that the sky is blue has not changed. No amount of science is going to undermine how you have experienced the sky on every cloudless day of your life. Though science has sowed a seed of doubt in your head, your belief remains that the sky is ultimately blue.

The sky is blue because of how you experienced it, and thus, you have manifested it so.

Your senses take precedence over physical reality. A violet sky is irrelevant to how you see the world.

Emotions and feelings are outside the venue of scientific explanation. Science can explain where in the brain they originate, the chemical reactions involved but not what they really ARE. Science cannot tell you why you love blue skies or what love is. They must be experienced.

Emotions and feelings can only be experienced. Science cannot quantify them to a causal root; they are purely manifested by your experiences.

At the root of emotions and feelings is the question of where they emanate from.

Science tells us that the violet sky emanates from the electromagnetic waves of light that emanate from the sun and is misinterpreted as blue by our eyesight.

Emotions and feelings cannot be explained by science.

Psychology is a branch of science that studies the human mind and behaviors and comes closest to the seat of their emanation. But psychology only goes so far down the rabbit hole and cannot explain the causal root of emotions or feelings.

Thus, we turn to religion to 'spell out' what emotions and feelings are. The scientific method is replaced by storytelling and symbolism.

An apple takes on a new meaning in the Bible. It becomes a symbol of knowledge, temptation, and the fruit of a lost paradise.

Religion tells us that emotions and feelings emanate from a Creator; in whose image we are created. Religions offer no unified composite description of a Creator, let alone any first-hand data of a Spiritual Deity. Each religion has its own variation on the theme that the Creator is positive, and a path exists to an afterlife.

Every major religion is based on the emotions and feelings demonstrated by the actions of people who they believe emulated the Most High. We generally call those people religious prophets.

Christianity, as noted, is the only exception in that it goes a step further and 'christened' Jesus as Divine.

This is where one's faith enters the picture. Traditional faith is the belief in written doctrine to understand emotions and feelings experienced in living this physical existence.

Faith in Divine Awareness has no written doctrines. It is a marriage of two worlds. The world of the physical and the world of the metaphysical. It is simply a channel through which to reflect one's experiences against the light of the Divine.

The concept of Divine Awareness is neither a religion nor a science but incorporates both.

Using Awareness is a path to experience the spiritual light of one's beliefs.

We hold beliefs in both worlds. Our collective knowledge of the physical world, via observation and the written word, has taught us much about the how, why, and what. It has enabled us to manipulate the physical world to our advantage.

Our collective knowledge of the spiritual world of emotions and feelings, via observation and the written word, has taught us much about the how, why, and what. It has enabled us to manipulate the spiritual world to our advantage.

Beliefs held in the workings of the physical realm can be quantifiably proven. Beliefs in the workings of the physical realm are uniformly accepted.

Beliefs held in the spiritual realm cannot be quantifiably proven. Beliefs in the spiritual realm are qualified individually from within.

In the Star Trek episode earlier described, we learned that overcoming a false reality, no matter how real it appears, can be accomplished. In the Star Trek episode, it required absolute faith, without an iota of doubt.

In our world of physical and emotional relativities, it is impossible to have absolute faith in anything without an iota of doubt. Unless you are Mr. Spock, Jesus, or the Buddha, it is beyond our capabilities.

Finally, rote recapitulation of Scripture will only take one so far in one's quest to the Divine. One must experience one's belief. Acting on and experiencing one's belief is the path to Divine Awareness.

Be it kind acts on a grandiose or minuscule scale, it does not matter. What matters is the quality of the act. Altruism is the highest motivation of any act and most resembles the ways of the Most High.

Using the principles of Divine Awareness is a powerful tool to EXPERIENCE emotions, feelings, and actions.

It adds certainty, removes doubt, and thus strengthens your beliefs.

The Realm of All Possibility

'Readers haven't heard much about it, but they will.

Quantum technology turns reality upside down.'

Michael Crichton

Quantum physics has taught us that what once seemed impossible is possible.

It has taught us that possible different outcomes can exist simultaneously. It has taught us the very nature of observation can influence outcomes. That reality is a two-way street. That reality both influences and can be influenced.

Quantum physics points to a monistic interpretation of the universe. That spiritual elements are not contrived thoughts apart from physical reality but are the essence of all Creation that our beliefs are both influenced and can influence.

If we apply the principles of the quantum world to the spiritual world, the existence of Divine Awareness can thus be PROVEN. Well, at least proven to the standard of 'a preponderance of evidence.'

When we visualize Divine Awareness through our own Awareness, we are visualizing elements of a Creator in our consciousness. The process of doing so requires energy. Thus, we are manifesting divine thoughts with the energy of our conscious minds.

Manifesting any thought is much like an apple seed. Within the seed, the essence of the apple is contained. Within the thought, the essence of a representation is contained.

Thoughts are compiled into a seed of a belief. Beliefs are then planted and grow. Just as the apple seed manifests as an apple tree, thoughts manifest from the essence contained in the thought.

Thoughts can manifest in the physical world, anywhere within the spectrum of negativity and positivity. Just as an apple tree can thrive, struggle, or die, so too is the fate of thoughts once planted.

All thoughts exist in the realm of all possibilities.

All outcomes are a matter of probability.

The more positive thoughts that are manifested, the more positive outcomes become probable.

Therein lies the power of positive thinking. The power of Divine Awareness.

Twenty Watts

"Everything is energy, and that is all there is to it. Match the frequency of the reality you want, and you cannot help but get that reality." Albert Einstein

The laws of thermodynamics tell us that energy can neither be created nor destroyed. It can only change states. Energy is matter without mass. The universe is a closed system with respect to energy. The same amount of energy exists in the universe today as existed at the time of the Big Bang.

At rest, the human body consumes approximately the same amount of energy as a 20-watt light bulb. At death, the energy within you is dispersed. While a biologist might tell you the dispersion is through heat and your energy being consumed by bacteriological processes, this does not account for the energy that is your consciousness or the essence of who you are. Humans are highly sentient beings and self-aware. This awareness surely requires energy in life. The departed spirit at death likely requires a similar energy not covered by biologic explanation.

If you have ever been exposed to the moment of death, the exit of one's spirit is undeniable. At the moment of my dad's death, I felt him depart, and the second he left his body, it was apparent his corpse was an empty shell. It is quite an amazing moment when your awareness (spirit) transitions to an afterlife.

A physicist would offer a much different explanation than a biologist as to where energy transfers as death. The following are the words of a quantum physicist, Dr Aaron Friedman, via an NPR interview:

"You want a physicist to speak at your funeral. You want the physicist to talk to your grieving family about the conservation of energy so they will understand that your energy has not died. You want the physicist to remind your sobbing mother about the first law of thermodynamics; that no energy gets created in the universe, and none is destroyed.

You want your mother to know that all your energy, every vibration, every Btu of heat, every wave of every particle that was her beloved child remains.

With her in this world. You want the physicist to tell your weeping father that amid energies of the cosmos, you gave as good as you got.

And at one point, you'd hope that the physicist would step down from the pulpit and walk to your brokenhearted spouse there in the pew and tell her that all the photons that ever bounced off your face, all the particles whose paths were interrupted by your smile, by the touch of your hand, hundreds of trillions of particles, have raced off like children, their ways forever changed by you.

And as your widow rocks in the arms of a loving family, may the physicist let her know that all the photons that bounced from you were gathered in the particle detectors that are her eyes, that those photons created within her constellations of electromagnetically charged neurons whose energy will go on forever.

You can hope your family will examine the evidence and satisfy themselves that the science is sound and that they will be comforted to know your energy's still around. According to the law of the conservation of energy, not a bit of you is gone; you are just less orderly."

Thus, the disbursement of energy in life and death can be looked at in three ways.

1. The energy you emit in the world has various influences on others and is passed along through them.
2. Biologic explanation of death… that your energy is dispersed as heat and is absorbed by bacteria.
3. Quantum Physics explanation of death…, that the energy of your essence lives on in a less orderly form of matter than a physical being.

I believe if you put all three explanations together, you have a complete explanation to account for the disbursement of one's 'wattage' in life and death.

So, in a nutshell....

Energy is energy. Matter is energy. Whether we exist as energy or energy configured as matter....it does not really matter. We are energy and exist, with purpose. The purpose being to make the Cosmos a better place, through acts of love and kindness. It's that simple. ....and all that matters.

Vessels of Photons

'Let there be light.'

Genesis 1:4

It is said we are created in God's image. That image is light. We are vessels designed to receive the light of Divine Awareness, God's essence.

The essence of light in the physical realm is a photon. Photons are the causal root of light. Light is a causal root of life. We are vessels designed to 'receive photons.' Vessels designed to receive light. All matter receives light.

The sun emits photons that illuminate the Earth in light. Photons originate in the Sun's core. The photons are born via nuclear fusion when cores of hydrogen smash together to make helium. Photons are a byproduct of this reaction.

When a photon is received in matter, its primary effect is absorbed by the electron of an atom, creating a positive charge. The photon is thus absorbed and dissipates. Photons are received at our core.

The relationship between an individual's Awareness and Divine Awareness is analogous to a photon's relationship to the sun. A photon is the tiniest essence of light. The sun is the Infinite essence of light on Earth.

Photons are the basic building blocks of light. Thus, the photon contains the essence of Light. Within the essence of Divine Awareness, knowledge of all things is contained. Photons are the carriers of that knowledge. The means by which Divine Awareness gives knowledge for our Awareness to receive.

Photons are how we communicate with the Divine.

Divine Communication

'We can become a channel and let ourselves be divinely led' Catherine Carrigan.

In my analogy, photons are the means of transmission of communication with the Divine. Photons are thus the 'language' of the Divine. Awareness.

All things are born with innate abilities to receive and process Awareness.

Awareness is the Great Teacher.

Divine Awareness teaches plants to be aware of their surroundings.

Divine Awareness teaches an ant to communicate with other ants.

Divine Awareness teaches a fish to fear.

Divine Awareness teaches a dog to feel love and a gamut of emotions.

Divine Awareness likewise teaches us a gamut of emotions but on a different, perhaps higher, frequency.

Humans have a powerful innate capacity to plug into Awareness. That capacity is housed within the 'third eye.' In Hinduism it is said to have the ability of vision and clairvoyance. It is said to possess mystical qualities when activated, a sixth sense.

The third eye is speculated to be linked to the pineal gland. It is thought to be a window to a higher level of consciousness, but there is no scientific evidence that it actually exists. Science likewise offers no explanation for the existence of consciousness in general. That is because the third eye and consciousness do not exist in time and space, just as Divine Awareness exists beyond time and space. The third eye is a spiritual concept.

The 'reality' of the third eye is that there is nothing mysterious about it. The third eye is the innate frequency within all people to receive Divine knowledge. One simply has to make a conscious effort to open one's Self to Awareness and listen to the 'telepathic transmissions' of Knowledge. There is nothing mystical about it. The third eye is a 'muscle'.... The more you use it, the stronger it gets.

The third eye is the spiritual means through which we communicate with the Divine.

Putting the Divine to work

'In love, a divine self-manifests.'

Lailah Gifty Akita

Knowledge is not something that is meant to be hoarded. Knowledge is meant to be shared and used. Divine knowledge is meant to be shared and used.

Divine Knowledge is innately good. Like water, it is powerful yet humble. It nurtures all things it encounters. It exists in a dynamic state and is adaptable. While sometimes it can manifest in a negative way, it is innately positive. It is innately positive because we can overcome its negative manifestations but cannot exist without its positive manifestations.

Photons are like droplets of water. They fill our vessels with knowledge. On a rudimentary basis, our vessels receive what we need to sustain. We grow only when our relationship with the Divine grows.

Growth can be stymied by the clouds in life. Tragedy, depression, greed, and misplaced love are examples of these clouds Clouds block the light and our ability to fill our vessels. The third eye closes.

When the third eye is kept open, we fill our vessels with the optimum nutrients to grow. To grow, we must use the knowledge we receive. We first listen. Then, we observe. We then seek the positives in our observations. We then manifest our thoughts and actions based on the positive aspects of what we process through our senses.

Properly recognizing and manifesting positivity in our thoughts and actions is emulating the Divine.

Emulating the Divine is OUR ULTIMATE PURPOSE

Using Awareness

'The key to growth is the introduction of higher dimensions of consciousness into our awareness.' Lao Tzu

There is no right or wrong way to use Awareness. Your Awareness operates on your own unique frequency, depending on how you are vested in the physical world. The clarity of your frequency is directly correlated with your perspective of Life. Perspective is based on the positivities and negativities you have been presented with and how you manifest them.

Positivity increases the strength of your frequency. Negativity reduces the strength of your frequency. But negativity, which is overcome, is the highest enhancer of all.

So here are a few of my personal thoughts on using Awareness.

Be your Self

Dig deep beneath the surface of your concerns.

Try and uncover the causal root of your concerns.

Remember, positivity is stronger than negativity.

Use doubt to confirm certainty.

Awareness is always accessible.

Create a personal means to summon awareness.

Examples…

Focus on the white noise in your head.

Focus on and visualize your third eye.

Create your own prayer to call on your Awareness,

Use a simple chant like "Please, Lord, open my eye to your light"

Keep your chant or prayer known only to your Awareness.

Understand Awareness is rarely instantaneous

Divine Awareness is awesome! Nothing to fear at all, especially if your beliefs and actions are aligned with positivity.

There are no negatives attached to Divine Awareness. Divine Awareness is not vengeful, jealous, egotistical, hateful, or moved to anger. All negativity in the physical realm is only manifested to enhance our understanding of positivity.

The more you summon Awareness, the more accessible it becomes.

Be patient and relinquish control to Awareness.

Trust your Awareness. After all, it is the essence of who you are.

Awareness will not always provide direct answers. Insights do not always follow a straight line, but they often lead you to a revelation or epiphany.

Prioritize Awareness over your physical reality. Filter your physical reality through Awareness before manifesting your actions.

Overlay your Being over your daily manifested self

(i.e., your 'work self', 'your social self,' 'your family self' etc.)

Sometimes, awareness will immediately guide your response; sometimes, it will only be an observer. But inevitably, it will enhance your perceptions and improve your actions and results.

Chapter 4

When The Curtain Closes

Death is not death

Life is pleasant. Death is pleasant. It is the transition that is troublesome.

Isaac Asimov

Death is uncomfortable on a lot of levels. It is a complete disruption of routine. It is a total disconnect from space and time. Death is an event that our minds file in denial until it draws near.

Death is draped in a fear of the unknown. Our only armament against death is faith. Faith is a belief. Faith is a product of our conscious mind when filtered through Awareness. As noted, it requires 'a leap'.

Death is the transition from the mind/body world to the world of Awareness.

Those with faith do not view death as a finite end but rather a natural transition. Energy never dies; it only changes form. All that is left of you is the energy of your inner Self, your inner consciousness. The universe of time and space has dissolved, and you are now in the universe of Divine Awareness.

At birth, your life began with a divine spark of light. That spark grew.

You physically evolved, and your beliefs evolved as well.

At death, the spark has been released, and you now exist as light in a universe of your beliefs.

Like in the Big Bang, your universe is no longer a solid block of matter. Death has freed your Awareness into a new universe of your own design, based on your beliefs, your essence.

In Divine Awareness, size no longer matters. You now exist in a world where quantum behaviors are front and center. Your energy is free to move about time and space without restriction. You can travel through light years of time instantaneously. You can experience superpositions and can occupy all possible states at the same time. You can be an infant, child, teen, young man, or old man... all at once. Your abilities to manifest refine as your beliefs adjust and learn the parameters of your new reality.

Your Awareness is much like a self-contained universe. Your universe is a product of your beliefs. You are the creator of your universe. Your universe is one of an infinite number of universes. Your Awareness is like a quantum entity within the entity of Divine Awareness.

In the Afterlife, reality is what you manifest reality to be.

Let us use a born-again Christian friend for example. Let us call him Fred.

Fred is now dead. Dead Fred has manifested Heaven as his next reality. Is it an eternal reality? What are its parameters? Who knows? What follows death is pure speculation.

Let's speculate. Heaven is the manifested beliefs of Fred. Being born again, the basic requisites of his beliefs are specific. Heaven is segregated to only those of the Christian faith. Furthermore, it is only for those whose Awareness has fully accepted Jesus as personal savior. Heaven is God's dwelling place. To Fred, it is something akin to a Sistine Chapel mural. By Fred's definition, Heaven is where kindred spirits reside, pray, and worship God's glory. Fred will be given a new body., like the Christ when resurrected. According to Scripture, Fred will bask in joy, dance, and sing and will live without a care in the world. Heaven is eternal; Fred has escaped all earthly bonds. Reincarnation is not an issue.

Heaven sounds glorious. But I wonder. Can Fred's loved ones who did not accept Jesus as their personal savior come and visit? Is the belief in Jesus as a personal savior the only belief that will manifest itself? What about all the rest of Fred' beliefs? Surely Fred had beliefs not totally congruent with Jesus's teachings, as well as beliefs that Jesus never broached. It is all rather perplexing to me.

Now, I by no means wish to patronize my Christian friends. The parables of Jesus are some of the finest works recorded by humankind. Are they the actual verbatim words of a divine entity? It is my belief they are not. But that is just my belief. We are all free to manifest our beliefs as we like.

The biggest sticking point I have with Christianity is the concept of Heaven being a binary choice between 'believers' and 'non-believers.' Either you fully accept Jesus as your personal savior, or you do not. Like traditional computing, 0 or 1 are your only options.

Rather than a binary choice, I believe an afterlife offers a realm of possibilities beyond 0 or 1. An afterlife more attuned to quantum computing, where all possibilities that reflect the Divine can coexist. I believe that the Divine can manifest more than a single 'heaven' scenario. That even the concept of pure potentiality (nothingness) is possible.

As for the actual existence of Heaven or any afterlife, I believe a preponderance of evidence can be determined: that it is more likely than not that an Afterlife exists. As for the specifics of daily life in an Afterlife, it is pure speculation. I write my thoughts on life in Heaven for entertainment value only. Though I truly hope for Fred's sake, Heaven is all that he hoped it would be; his manifestations are not mine.

Let us now speculate on a Buddhist afterlife. Our friend Aang (the name translated means peaceful, soaring) has ascended from earthly bonds. Aang's beliefs are centered on Enlightenment and have little concern for what an afterlife will bring. What will be, will be. For Aang, an afterlife is most likely transitional. He believes there are realms of existence based on one's achieved wisdom and compassion. Only when one achieves the highest level of both will one break the chains of reincarnation and dwell in a Divine world of Essence. The world of 'Nothingness.' The original realm from which all Creation emanates.

Aang's belief system seems much harder to achieve than Fred's. Fred's path is one of submission to accepting Christ as a personal savior and becoming one with the body of Christ.

Aang's path appears quite different, though the goal is the same, namely, to become one with wisdom and compassion.

If you ask me, both paths lead to the same destination.

Manifest Destiny

It's my manifest destiny to wear a dress in every country
Eddie Izzard

An example of manifest destiny was the idea that white Americans were ordained to settle the entire continent of North America. It was God's plan. A plan to displace and destroy Native Americans. A treatise by settlers to justify taking what was 'Divinely given.'

Clearly, this manifest destiny was a cruel, false doctrine to justify brutality, completely opposite of the underlying doctrines of their Christian faith.

Religious dogma can be a mixed bag.

The only true manifest destiny in life is death.

In both birth and death there are an infinite number of possible outcomes. Life is much like quantum computing, where 0 and 1 are not the only outcomes. Where one can have more than a binary choice. Where outcomes are a matter of probabilities of various combinations of 0 and 1, and all points in between.

And though physical death is a certainty, an afterlife is uncertain. Logically, if death is a continuum of a birth/life/afterlife cycle, it would seem an afterlife, as in life, would offer infinite outcomes... An infinite combination of metaphysical alchemy free of space and time.

Manifesting Beliefs

'I got to get into it before I get out of it.

And I got to get out of it before I get into it.'

Frank Zappa

I think Frank got it right. Frank inadvertently reduced the chasm between Eastern religious doctrine and Western religious doctrine to two sentences.

The original context of Frank's words was from a song (Dynamo Hum), offering a humorous explanation about lovemaking. Specifically, he was referring to the process of how he could invoke an orgasm out of his partner. But Frank stumbled on something quite deep.

The first sentence, 'I got to get into it before I get out of it,' is a reflection on Western doctrine. In Western doctrine, one must live one's life to create a Self that reflects the attributes of the Creator. In Christianity, for example, one must become part of the body of Christ. In Christianity accepting Christ is the only choice to salvation. You are presented with a binary choice…yes for Heaven, no for Hell.

The second sentence, 'I got to get out of it before I get into it,' is a reflection on Eastern doctrine. In Eastern doctrine, one must remove one's Self to become part of a whole. In Buddhism, for example, wholeness is the ultimate attribute of the Creator. In Buddhism, it is not entirely a binary choice. If you do not achieve selflessness, you are reincarnated and get to try again.

I guess the only question that remains is what is 'it.' In Frank's context, 'it' is a mutual orgasm. In both Eastern and Western doctrine, it is likewise the attainment of mutual love, joy, and happiness. 'It' is the attainment of oneness. It is thus congruent within both Eastern and Western religious contexts.

How one manifests 'it' thus becomes a question of whether one follows a path of developing Selfhood or a path of relinquishing Selfhood. Which path is the proper path becomes the question.

Whichever one follows is simply a manifestation of the possibilities that Divine Awareness leads one toward. If you must determine which path is the 'true' path, you would be wise to consider the reality of quantum computations.

In traditional computing a bit can represent either a 0 or a 1, but not represent both simultaneously.

Traditional computing represents the relativities of the physical world. In the physical world, there are many binary choices. Right or wrong, love or hate…. a positive aspect vs a negative aspect. Much like Christianity's position on accepting Jesus. Everything or nothing.

In quantum computing, qubits can represent both 0 and 1 simultaneously and all probabilities in between.

Quantum computing represents the relativities of the spiritual world. In the spiritual world, all things are possible. Much like Buddhism, one has many possible choices. Aside from attaining the Divine by totally ridding oneself of Selfhood and breaking the chains of reincarnation, it is okay to keep trying. There is no ultimate negative consequence.

Of course, the choice is yours. I love Jesus, but I am just not comfortable with the notion of a 'segregated country club' manifestation of Heaven. I also love the Buddhist teachings of humility and selflessness. Personally, I'm going with quantum logic and following a probability in between.

In a quantum mindset, the paths of selfhood, non-selfhood, or any possibility in between can be manifested.

The Near-Death Experience

"We are conscious not because of the brain, but in spite of it."

Dr Larry Dossey

My near-death experience (NDE) was a life-changing moment for me. Was my brain just playing tricks on me? Was it just an elixir of chemical secretions in my brain to combat a physical trauma? Perhaps. Or had I begun a departure into the next world? Were the shackles of time and space being released and the door to the afterlife opening? Perhaps.

Regardless…. My NDE was a life-changing event for me.

Regardless of scientific explanation, Life changing events are real because they really change who you are.

My NDE was both vivid and powerful. It is extremely hard to give an accurate representation of something that I perceived to have occurred beyond the parameters of outside space and time. Poetic form I believe, is the best representation.

The River

It had rained for a week straight.

At times torrential.

The once gentle trickle of the creek,

Raged with power and ferocity.

The creek flowed into the River.

Where the waters gained momentum.

Unlike the loud crackle of the creek,

The River flowed with an almost silent momentum.

The creek being analogous to a powerful man,

The River, being a great behemoth,

We rafted down the powerful creek,

The three of us Frank, Jim and I.

H.L. Sawyer

It was only after we entered the behemoth,

Did Frank mention, "Hey, I can't swim

Jim and I, being half Frank's age, could only chuckle,

At Frank's misgiving at such a point of no return.

The River had already grabbed us in its powerful grasp,

And there was no turning back from our point of entry.

Through the first rapids, we shot,

We hit the 'V' through the rocks with pure precision.

With Jim in the back, Frank in the middle, and I in the front,

We whisked through like a slingshot.

With no one on the shore,

The River was ours alone.

The River hummed a steady, loud mantra,

A Eulogy to Cosmo

Like a Temple full of Buddhist monks chanting Om.

Like Jim, Frank, and I,

The River was alive and full of adrenaline.

But things were to quickly change,

As we hit the next set of rapids.

I was in the front,

And saw first what lay in store.

It was at least a five-foot drop,

And I was flung from the canoe like a feather.

How fast things had changed,

We had disrespected the River's power.

From that moment forward,

I have no sense of time.

H.L. Sawyer

I remember it was a cold, cloudy day,

My jeans, sweatshirt, and denim jacket weighed me down.

I remember Frank's cries for help,

Not panicked, but stoic and steady.

I remember trying to go after Frank,

But feeling the River pulling me down.

I remember Frank's cries growing fainter,

As he moved farther and farther away.

And then I remember a calmness came over me,

I was in either the darkness of the River or something else.

I remember my feet touching the bottom,

And I pushed off and glided upwar

A feeling of beauty and tranquility

Engorged my entire being.

A Eulogy to Cosmo

Unlike the River being engorged by the torrential rains,

I was engorged by a quietude and sense of awe.

For a brief moment, the veil of life had been lifted,

And all things revealed in an instant.

While beyond words or human perception,

For an instant, I was at One with All.

It was a religious feeling.

But beyond religious dogma,

So pure and so simple,

As if I was embraced in the pure love of my Creator.

As I rose up, I was floating,

But more like a feather than a drowning young man.

I looked up and saw a white light,

H.L. Sawyer

A pulsating brilliant light of a billion lumens.

It was the most spectacular light.

I had ever seen or felt.

It was pulling me to it,

As if I belonged and was part of it.

And then something happened,

I looked down and saw my lifeless body.

Floating spread eagle in the River's depth,

In complete juxtaposition to my spirit body.

Whether it was my inner voice,

Or the voice of a Higher Power, I do not know.

But the words, "You're 22, and it's not your time."

Resuscitated me like a defibrillator.

A Eulogy to Cosmo

In an instant, I was back in my body,

And broke through the surface of the water.

I swam with all my strength,

And negotiated across the current to the shore.

I was alive, as was Jim,

Who had made it to the New York side of the River

Delaware

When I made it to the Pennsylvania shore,

I stripped my heavy clothes off.

I ran down the shore,

Screaming for Frank.

I found him, I guess, about a mile downstream.

Exhausted but alive.

H.L. Sawyer

Frank was a thin but powerful man,

He looked like Mr. Zig Zag with Popeye's forearms.

He had managed to hang onto the capsized canoe,

With both strength and tenacity.

We all had survived our idiocy,

And disrespect for the river's power.

Only the next day did we learn,

Three other men had died on the River that day.

It was their time.

Freebird

If the birdcage becomes broken, the bird will continue to exist. Its feelings will be even more powerful, its perceptions greater, and its happiness increased.

Abdu'l Baha

When the body perishes, the spirit is set free. The dense world of the physical is lifted, and the world of Divine essence is revealed. The divine essence is the world of Divine Awareness. (Divine Awareness being God)

While our next world is beyond our ability to comprehend, again, we can have some fun and speculate.

In the next world, we are 'bodiless. Since there is no space or time, the laws of physics no longer apply. No more need for physical sustenance. The only sustenance needed is a connection to Divine light. We are infinitely smaller, yet infinitely larger. Tiny photons that can quantumly, manipulate time and space.

In the Afterlife, physical matter is opaque; feelings are now 'solid matter.' Feelings are now directly manifested.

We arrive much the same as a newborn. Our essence has been formed through our 'gestational' time on Earth. Our essence is

119

the product of our core beliefs. Our core beliefs are the product of our conscious beliefs filtered through our individual eyes of Awareness.

Perhaps the afterlife (the world of Divine Essence) is much like a quantum world. You are no longer a baby, a child, an adult, or a senior citizen. You are only that Being that experienced all your physical manifestations on Earth. But the good news is you can be any manifestation of your Being at any 'time' you wish. You can be 'young you' and 'old you' simultaneously! You are simply you.

As you might imagine, Divine Essence is quite a different realm. While you are in a closer presence to the Divine, you probably don't have front-row seats. While you have assumed the image of Divine Awareness and are now yourself, light, you are a tiny photon. Your Awareness is a quantum image of Divine Awareness.

In the world of Divine Essence, one is given as one has the ability to receive. Your ability to receive is based on how much Awareness you have incorporated into your conscious mind beliefs

Let us use Mother Teresa as an example. Mother Teresa selflessly treated everyone with great compassion and without preconditions. She spent her entire life helping the poorest of the poor. She stood in the face of starvation and disease, and never once did her faith blink,

A Eulogy to Cosmo

I think it is safe to say that Mother Teresa developed deep convictions based on her Awareness connection with Divine Awareness. The frequency at which she connected was far higher and deeper than most of humanity.

Mother Teresa's light of Divine Awareness shines brightly and thus can better comprehend the essence of the Divine. Her essence is much closer to Divine essence. Logically, her light occupies a close position to the Most High.

As a Catholic, she has manifested her Heaven 'within the body of Christ.' Her position within Christ's body is in the highest frequency of Light.

The concept of an Afterlife has infinite variations. Each Afterlife is manifested based on one's beliefs. Each Afterlife maintains a position relative to the frequency of light that one has attained.

Looking at it conceptually, the Divine world is like a college campus. Christian Heaven is but one building on the Afterlife campus. On the top floor, are housed Ph.D. candidates (Mother Teresa), and on the bottom floor are incoming freshmen. There are many other buildings on the campus.

In Divine Essence, there is no Hell. Only degrees of light. As previously discussed, negativity does not exist beyond the physical world of relativity. Death frees us from the negative ends of equations. There is no longer hate, only love. It is simply not logical to believe hate would exist in the presence of an Almighty Loving God.

It is impossible to hate in the light of Divine Essence.

You experience things as they really are, without physical limitations. The world is a very different place. Your senses are acute to the essence of all things. The sky is violet.

In the realm of Divine Essence, we begin a new journey. Our new journey is not so much to differentiate between love and hate but to hone our understanding of love. To learn love's levels. To learn all levels of positivity.

There are many realms within the realm of Divine Essence. It's a 'big place.' The higher the realm one occupies depends on one's ability to comprehend positivities such as love. How bright your individual light of Awareness shines determines what realm you exist in. Your realm is populated with other 'photons' of similar brightness (Awareness).

The lowest levels of the realm of Divine Essence are thus inhabited by those whose conscious beliefs and actions were guided by negativity. Their reality is dimly lit, but not a doomed one. Perhaps the lowest levels could be interpreted as 'Hellish.' But

Divine Awareness is not vindictive and has a forgiving nature. I would speculate that, somehow the negativity they carried forward can be overcome and a path to a higher light can be attained.

The highest levels of the realm of Divine Essence are thus inhabited by those whose conscious beliefs and actions were guided by positivity and used their Awareness to grow their connection with Divine Awareness. The higher the level of attainment, the closer one approaches the pure essence of the Creator.

So, there you have it. My manifestation of my Afterlife. A universe where God is the great light, and I am a photon. I maintain a position relative to God. It is based on the intensity of my light relative to God's. The feelings and beliefs I developed on Earth determine who and where I am. They are my starting point. My Being is now in a new state of infancy in a new reality.

My new purpose in life is to further enhance my light. To move closer to the light, with the ultimate goal to become one with the Divine. For my Awareness to mirror that of the Divine's.

Ultimately, the end game of all religions is to become one with the Light of Creation, be it Allah, God, the Father, the Son, and the Holy Ghost, Vishnu. Shiva, and Brahma or Nothingness.

I see old friends and family. I make new friends. I seek

interactions with 'like-minded photons'. Perhaps there are even 'photons' from other life forms! After all, the universe is a big place. Maybe I could make friends with the Melkotians! (How cool would that be!) There is enough variation to make life enjoyable. My new world is like a dream. But unlike a dream, the light of Divine Awareness is much more accessible. Only the negative polarities I carried forward from the material world limit my connection to Divine essence.

I can now manifest my thoughts and feelings. At first, this new reality is daunting. My friends and family that have come before me, nurture my adjustment. I eventually learn how to manipulate my inner world driven reality. The negativity I carried forward from the past world dissipates. Through the four stages of learning, I eventually learn to manifest my new reality effortlessly.

Life is happier and better in my new world of consciousness.

But what happened to Dead Fred and Ang? Are they in a higher realm than I am? I don't know, and it is not my concern. But if I had to place a wager, I'd bet we have each attained a reality of our own making, within the confines of Divine Awareness.

For as Jesus said, "the kingdom of God is within you."

And I can run with that!

Oceans...A Closing Thought

Water always goes where it wants to go, and nothing in the end can stand against it.... Margaret Atwood

In closing, I wish it were possible to present you with a quantifiable 'unified theory' for Divine Awareness. But such is not possible in the realm of time/space relativity. We exist in a juxtaposition between the physical and the spiritual...A twilight zone between external and internal perceptions. Where fixed objects appear solid, and thoughts, feelings, and beliefs appear opaque.

Perhaps in the Afterlife, things will reverse. A realm that I mentioned, where fixed objects will appear opaque, and thoughts, feelings, and beliefs will appear solid. A realm where true Essence is revealed. Until then, I would like to leave you with a final thought, and best wishes that you find all that you seek.

Oceans

The essence of an ocean

Is a single droplet of water

When it rains

Droplets of water are dispersed.

From the highest mountain,

To the levels of the sea

Water is omnipresent.

Even in the most arid desert

Water flows humbly,

From the Most High to the low

Water forms puddles

Puddles form streams

Streams form creeks

Creeks form rivers

Rivers form lakes

And the oceans

Depending on the origin and path

Droplets of water manifest in different ways

Water is patient.

It initially seeks the path of least resistance.

Water is nurturing.

It nurtures all things in its path.

Water is strong.

It flows over rocks,

Which bow to its strength,

And are smoothed by its flow.

Awareness is like water.

It begins as a single droplet and can expand without limits.

Awareness is humble,

It is patient.

It is nurturing.

It is strong.

Divine Awareness is like an ocean.

Infinite in its humility, patience

Nourishment and strength

Like droplets of water in a great ocean

We are all part of a great essence

And that great essence is the Divine.

Chapter 5

Visualizations

In this writing, I highlighted many thoughts. Each thought being manifested by a string of preceding thoughts designed to make a point.

As in life, there is always a story behind the story. Below are the highlighted points of my story. They are the story behind my story…my key points to visualizing Awareness.

I offer this work as a manual to consider the belief that Awareness is the foundation of who you really are. That your Awareness is linked to a Divine Awareness of a higher power. By recognizing and using this conceptual connection you can refine the quality of your beliefs and improve your life and the lives of others.

Quantum physics casts doubt on the certainty of all our core beliefs.

Casting doubt on one's beliefs builds certainty in true beliefs.

In order to accept a religion/belief system, one must start somewhere.

Faith is the basic assumption upon which beliefs are built.

Beliefs and actions are the building blocks of who and what we really are.

Divine Awareness are the thoughts of God. All knowledge is generated by the thoughts of God.

Awareness is the interplay of individual consciousness with Divine Awareness.

Accessing Awareness is more than a prayer, it is a conversation.

Quantum entanglements defy space and time, as well as logic. How can particles influence each other instantaneously over light years of space?

Could there be a cosmic entity that connects us to the Universe and beyond? An energy that exists beyond our perceptions that defies linear logic. A direct frequency to the Divine, whose only encumbrance is the density of the physical world, relegating the Divine to a faint voice within. As in quantum physics, a cosmic entanglement, not between photons but rather Awarenesses, that can communicate over infinite distances instantaneously.

Awareness is the entanglement between consciousness

and the Divine.

Consciousness and Awareness are partners in a quantum entanglement.

Everyone and all things have a unique frequence (ability) to connect with Divine Awareness.

Awareness is that small white noise you hear in your mind...the third eye. The voice of intuition, creativity, clairvoyance. Consciousness/Awareness is who you are!

The energy of love is every bit as real as the energy from the sun that paints the sky violet.

The more we open our Awareness to that of the Divine, the more the clouds of negativity dissipate in our lives.

Life exists on a razor thin edge, and it is awesome that we even exist.

Negatives are all creations of the physical world, so we can understand the positives of the higher realm.

It is the higher purpose of living to learn to qualify negativity as subservient to positivity. To recognize that love exists on a higher plan than hate.

The premise of all religious doctrine requires a leap of faith to subscribe to one's beliefs.

Divine Awareness requires a leap of faith as a path to clarity of one's beliefs. It is a complement to one's beliefs.

Divine Awareness is a path to a deeper personal relationship with a Higher Power.

It is only my inner Being that has remained a constant. It is my inner Being who has witnessed who I was, I am, and am yet to be.

AWARENESS IS WHO I AM. AWARENESS IS WHO YOU ARE.

Living in Awareness is simply a commitment to reprioritize one's thinking.

It is as simple as changing your phone settings.

Living in Awareness requires little effort. It is the conscious act of manifesting the Divine in the moments of living. Once learned, it becomes an autonomic act.

How much a plant can feel is not fully understood. But plants can clearly experience sensations and are thus sentient.

To varying degrees, all life is sentient to some level or another.

To varying degrees, all life possesses some level of self-awareness.

To varying degrees, all life possesses some level of Divine Awareness.

Consciousness is a collection of mental attributes, thoughts, feelings, and beliefs.

When consciousness is filtered through Awareness, the essence of what all living things are becomes clearer.

Positivity is stronger than negativity. Love is stronger than hate.

Quantum mechanics demonstrates communication can occur in the physical world outside of space and time.

Thus, it is more feasible than not to assume our Awareness likewise has the ability to communicate with another Awareness outside the parameters of space and time.

Just as quantum computing has developed practical benefits beyond traditional computing, developing your frequency with Divine Awareness can likewise spawn practical benefits.

Opening your Awareness to Divine Awareness opens the door to the Observer Effect.

When actions occur in the light of Divine Awareness, the quality of your behaviors/outcomes naturally improve.

Religions are 'how to' guidebooks on how to lead a life

that will take you to an afterlife with a favorable outcome.

Religions throughout history have codified moral behaviors.

Religions throughout history have been a means of social control and have been intolerant of anything deemed contrary to their teachings. Intolerance is contrary to Divine Awareness. Therefore, religion can be manifested improperly.

Christianity, Islam, and Judaism all offer a continuation of a Selfhood afterlife based on varying degrees of deeds and faith in a Deity.

Hinduism and Buddhism, on the other hand, believe life is a cycle that can only be broken by relinquishment of Selfhood.

A commonality with Western religions is that specific parameters of an Afterlife are predefined and binary in nature.

It is possible that in an Afterlife, there may be no specific predefined parameters much like in quantum computing where 0 and 1 and all possibilities in between can exist simultaneously.

Divine Awareness is compatible with both spiritualism and all religions.

Regardless of religious doctrine, what matters is that you manifest positivity.

Religious doctrines that manifest positivity are all paths

to the same light.

Any religious tenet that is intolerant in nature is contrary to the nature of Divine will.

The mind exists neither in existence nor non-existence but between the two.

Eastern religious doctrine teaches emptying one's Self from the illusions of the material realm is the ultimate path to happiness. In its void, wise people create their own Heaven and fools their own Hell.

Reality is sometimes neither clear nor obvious in the eye or mind.

At its essence, reality is a projection that exists only when we believe in it.

Only in the Divine light of essence, can doubt be entirely lifted.

Without doubt there can be no certainty.

Doubt is our guide to Certainty.

Science can tell us much about what externally manifested things are but little about what is internally manifested.

Faith is not validated by science and can only be proven

by experience.

The concept of Divine Awareness is neither a religion nor a science but incorporates both.

Using Divine Awareness is a path to experience one's spiritual beliefs in the light of the divinity of one's own being.

Using the principles of Divine Awareness is a powerful tool to EXPERIENCE your emotions, feelings, and actions. It adds certainty, removes doubt, and thus strengthens one's beliefs.

All thoughts exist in the realm of all possibility.

All outcomes are a matter of probability.

The more positive thoughts that are manifested, the more positive outcomes become probable.

Energy is energy. Matter is energy. Whether we exist as energy or energy configured as matter...it doesn't matter. We are energy and exist with purpose. The purpose being to make the Cosmos a better place through acts of love and kindness. It's that simple, and all that matters.

'Photons' are how we communicate with the Divine.

The third eye is the physical means through which we

communicate with the Divine.

Properly recognizing and manifesting positivity in our thoughts and actions is emulating the Divine.

EMULATING THE DIVINE IS OUR ULTIMATE PURPOSE.

Overlay your inner Being over your daily manifested selves.

Death is the transition from the mind/body world to the world of Awareness.

At birth, your life began with a divine spark of light. That spark grew, you physically evolved, and your beliefs evolved as well.

At death, the spark has been released, and you now exist as light in a universe of your beliefs.

In the Afterlife, reality is what you manifest reality to be.

The only true manifest destiny in life is death.

And though physical death is a certainty, an afterlife is uncertain. Logically if death is a continuum of a birth/life/afterlife cycle, it would seem an afterlife, as in life, would offer infinite outcomes. ...An infinite combination of metaphysical alchemy free of space and time.

In traditional computing a bit can represent either 0 or 1, but not represent both simultaneously.

In quantum computing, qubits can represent both 0 and 1 simultaneously, and all probabilities in between.

Regardless of scientific explanation, life changing events are real because they really change who you are.

In the Afterlife, physical matter is opaque. Feelings are now 'solid matter'. Feelings can now be directly manifested.

It is impossible to hate in the light of Divine Essence.

Ultimately, the end game of all religions is to become one with the Light of Creation, be it God, Allah, the Father the Son and Holy Ghost, Vishnu, Shiva and Brahma or Nothingness.

Depending on origin and path, like droplets of water we manifest in different ways.

Awareness is like water; it begins as a single droplet and can expand without limit.

Divine Awareness is like an ocean. Infinite in its humility, patience, nourishment, and strength. Like droplets of water in a great ocean, we are all part of a great essence. And that great essence is the Divine.

Postscript

Thank you for sharing your time with me. I hope you enjoyed my speculations on life, love, and the pursuit of happiness. Perhaps you found all my vignettes enjoyable. Perhaps you found none to be enjoyable. Most likely, the net result was somewhere in between.

Regardless of whether you think I have hit upon something novel or am just full of crap, I hope at least in some small way, I cracked the door open to your curiosity.

Please keep in mind the sheer awesomeness of the Universe. Take the time to ponder its vastness, its tininess, its intricacies, its beauty, and its essence.

In pursuit of whichever path in life you choose to follow, keep in mind that you are more than a physical shell. That you are part of a greater whole. That your existence is meant to be more than the autonomic routines we all get stuck in. That your existence is truly miraculous! That life is a learning experience. And that one day your Inner Being will transcend time and space. And what you have learned is all the baggage you can take on your next journey.

I urge you to open your mind to Awareness. Just give it a try and be at one with your true Self; your divine Self... The being you truly are.

139

www.ingramcontent.com/pod-product-compliance
Lightning Source LLC
Chambersburg PA
CBHW050442150626
46551CB00028B/1105